# ROVER, *DON'T* ROLL OVER

# A COMPASSIONATE
## TRAINING GUIDE
### FOR DOGS
#### AND THEIR PEOPLE

# ROVER, *DON'T* ROLL OVER

## by **JODY ROSENGARTEN**
### of The Bark Stops Here

**TEN SPEED PRESS**
Berkeley | Toronto

Ten Speed Press
P.O. Box 7123
Berkeley, California
94707
www.tenspeed.com

Distributed in Australia by Simon and Schuster Australia, in Canada by Ten Speed
Press Canada, in New Zealand by Southern Publishers Group, in South Africa by Real
Books, and in the United Kingdom and Europe by Airlift Book Company.

Cover and Interior Design by Nancy Austin

Library of Congress Cataloging-in-Publication Data

Rosengarten, Jody.
Rover, don't roll over : a compassionate training guide for dogs and their people / Jody
Rosengarten of The Bark Stops Here.
    p. cm.
ISBN 1-58008-564-4
1. Dogs—Training. 2.Dogs—Behavior. I. Title.
SF431.R645 2004
636.7'0887—dc22
                2003027628

First printing, 2004

Printed in Canada
1 2 3 4 5 6 7 8 9 10 – 07 06 05 04

**To ReRun**

# CONTENTS

# Introduction

## Confessions of a Dog Trainer

My dogs sleep on my bed. They eat "people" food, lick me on the face, and occasionally precede me when walking through doors. There you have it. And, while I'm confessing, though they know how to heel precisely, sit straight, and even roll over, I rarely ask them to because it just seems silly.

I believe there are too many rules to dog training. Abiding by these rules is a turnoff, not to mention way too much work. "Always use his name *here*, never *there*," "Make eye contact," "Avoid eye contact," "Say 'off,' not 'down.'" And is it "leave it," "drop," or "phooey"? English is a dog's second language. I do this for a living and even I get confused.

*Rover, Don't Roll Over* is a pro-dog, anti-dogmatic manual that rejects the rigidity of traditional obedience training in favor of a kinder, gentler approach that delights in dogs' joie de vivre. It is written for the thinking person who wants to better understand what makes his dog tick. The puppy's perspective is always considered. This is a book for those who want a well-behaved dog but don't want to spend all of their free time getting him there.

The practical exercises taught here are broken down into simple steps. Suggestions for their real-life application honor your individuality and that of your dog. Both the first-time puppy owner and the longtime dog devotee will learn how to solve problems and address a dog's special needs. If you want to spoil your dog but you still want him to listen, *Rover, Don't Roll Over* is for you.

Living with a dog is like sharing a spectacular meal that goes on year after year with someone you adore. They are a gift to the soul. To fully appreciate all that your dog can be, please take the time to teach

3

him the basics contained in this book. Of equal importance, however, is being open to learning what dogs have to teach us. Dogs are the essence of authenticity; they are present, pure, and passionate. Like panning for gold, dogs have riches for us to uncover.

I believe that life is made more meaningful by dogs' inclusion in it. To respectfully integrate these chosen creatures into our world, it just makes sense that we better understand theirs. This is what *Rover, Don't Roll Over* is all about.

## Dogs Because . . .

I am a full-time dog trainer/behavior therapist and have run The Bark Stops Here since 1980. It was supposed to have been an interim thing until I figured out what I really wanted to do with my life. Little did I know. I have lost track of how many dogs I've worked with over the years, but during a good week, between group classes and house calls, I might work with fifty. Then there is my resident pack of three or four. Always rescued, my dogs are mostly mutts, or, as I prefer, "multiple pedigrees."

I have never lived a day of my life without at least one dog. I can more readily imagine living without legs than without dogs. As a child, despite trying desperately to fit in, I always felt different than the other kids. My family moved a lot; my parents got divorced when I was twelve (long before it was common); and I had numerous medical problems. The one constant presence throughout was the family dog. My love of dogs expanded to all animals, and I began collecting turtles, birds, frogs, and insects. Obsessed with Africa, I lived in Tanzania for more than a year as a teenager and started to write a book about my experience called *From Jewish Princess to African Queen*.

Although I was popular enough, I mostly wanted to be with my animals. I still do. That I have been able to parlay this passion into a career makes me one of the most privileged people I know. In Joseph Campbell's words, I pursued my bliss.

The dog, of course, is the focus of my work, but dogs typically take up only a small part of my energy. Dogs come easily to me; I get them, and feel what they feel. Many say this is a gift, but it can also be a curse. People require the real work. It's not that I am a human-hating animal person, but if a session stresses me out, it's rarely the dog's fault.

Mostly, however, I enjoy working with people. (Helping them to see things from their dog's point of view is where the challenge lies.) I often think of myself more as a mediator than a dog trainer. My goal is to preserve the puppy's joyfulness during training so that the puppy and his people get the most pleasure possible from one another. Some of my favorite clients are adults who fall in love with their first dog—born-again dog owners—I love showing them the way.

When I got started in New York City back in the Dark Ages of dog training, almost everyone else was so harsh and heavy-handed that my gentle approach was all but belittled. Now, twenty-three years later, the pendulum has swung so far in the other direction that the prevailing sentiment seems to be that one should never say no to a dog. I believe moderation is the way to go. (Perhaps "balance" is a better word.) Consequences matter.

This is the premise upon which the theory of operant conditioning is based. Operant, or Skinnerian, conditioning addresses the impact of consequences on voluntary behavior. This is what dog training is all about. A savvy teacher should first set the puppy up to succeed by encouraging his making the right choices and, if necessary, buffer the consequences of wrong choices so that the mildest correction possible is delivered, seemingly from the source itself. The operative word is "choice." The training trilogy is completed by immediately redirecting Rover back to the task at hand.

(It is vital to build up a puppy's confidence for his first six months. This is best accomplished through intensive socialization. Expose young Rover to a wide array of people, animals, sights, scents, sounds, and sensations.) Gently handle Rover all over. These experiences should be fun for the pup, as they will largely determine how he reacts to those things in the future. (Since fear is the number one reason that dogs bite, early socialization is essential.) It is easier to quell excesses later than it is to instill confidence after this critical developmental period. I strongly recommend that you take Rover to a puppy class. (Ask to observe a class prior to enrolling so that you can determine whether the instructor is gentle and positive.)

What about those of us who adopt mature dogs? Clearly, we've missed the early socialization boat and, tragically, should Rover have been intensely traumatized early on, this experience may be too firmly imprinted for him to be readily rehabilitated. But for many, late

5

socialization can still lead to great advances. At the very least the dog will associate these fun, new socialization experiences with you.

Fear of novel things is quite common with poorly socialized dogs. To remedy this, classical, or Pavlovian, conditioning comes into play. Very simply put, while operant conditioning deals with *actions,* classical conditioning addresses *emotions.* Using the classical concepts of desensitization and counterconditioning, you can slowly influence Rover's feelings. This is a subtle process whereby exposure to the dreaded object is incrementally increased (desensitization) and in its presence really great things happen (counterconditioning). So if the appearance of the once-terrifying umbrella-toting man wearing a hat means Rover is now given a burger, the dog may decide he is not so awful after all. Classical conditioning is at the core of many programs that address people's fear of flying and other phobias.

Having worked with thousands of dogs and their people over the past twenty-three years, I have come to appreciate that although there may be a finite number of dog issues, the relationship between each dog and his people is unique. What worked for your neighbor and her Akita may be totally inappropriate for your borzoi and you. Indeed, what worked with your last Lhasa apso may not work with your present one. Fixed formulas often fail. Nothing I nor anyone else recommends will succeed with every dog. As in all relationships, flexibility is essential. One size does not fit all.

If you haven't already noticed—be warned—unsolicited advice abounds. Everyone is an expert when it comes to your puppy. I paid a house call recently to a woman with a seven-week-old shepherd mix named Drifter. When I arrived the puppy was wearing a choke collar that she had purchased at her mother's recommendation so that she would be "ready" for me. Not only do I no longer use choke collars, but even when I did, I never put one on a puppy under four months old. Their delicate little tracheas can easily collapse, causing irreversible damage or even death. She had also been advised by a friend to smack Drifter with a rolled-up newspaper when he had an "accident." But there's no such thing as an accident when you're only seven weeks old. Smacking a puppy is like spanking an infant for peeing in her diapers, simply terrorizing the puppy for something over which he has no control. That first session, like so many others, was more about undoing the damage caused by well-intentioned others than about teaching anything new. When in doubt, always err on the side of gentleness. You may not get the desired result, but at least you won't create any problems that require fixing in the future. Consider it our Hippocratic oath: First do no harm.

Living with dogs provides us with an opportunity to share our lives intimately with members of another species, like accessible ETs. Because dogs have to accommodate themselves to our culture, they often have to subjugate aspects of their own. It's inevitable, then, that certain bumps will be encountered along the way. Puppies have no innate knowledge of the difference between an antique wooden chair and a brand new stick, or between a rawhide bone and a leather sandal. They're dogs, not Bob Barker. For them, the price is always right. Frankly, I'm amazed that most dogs transition into our world as well as they do. Yes, puppies are a lot of work, but I believe it's a small price to pay for all that they give over their lifetimes.

## What Dogs Do

I don't know about you, but I would rather know what to expect up front than be caught off guard. Just tell me if it's going to hurt, how long it will take, or what it costs so that I'm prepared. Here, then, is the truth about dogs: Dogs jump and dig and bark. Most shed. They roll in stinky stuff and sometimes even eat it. Deer droppings, a.k.a. "trail mix," are a favorite at my house. Puppies will chew almost anything, and they pee and poop often and everywhere. Then, of course, some bite. There you have it, the down and dirty of dogs.

It is estimated that one out of two dogs acquired is kept by his original person. *Only one out of two.* This breaks my heart. Dog ownership is not for everyone. So rather than romanticize what it's like to live with one, I thought you should know what they do right off the bat. Your canine caveat emptor. Having said that, the one thing that dogs do that makes everything worthwhile is warm your heart in a way little else in life can. A dog is as close to a universal gift of love as you get.

Over the past decade or so dog training has been elevated to a more enlightened, sophisticated level than ever before, thanks in large part to the Association of Pet Dog Trainers. Regrettably, though, there are still many out there who become trainers because of their need to control and dominate. Who better to boss around than a dog?

7

Control for control's sake can be a treacherous thing and is the stuff of bullies and bigots. Most of us have control issues: We may have too much or too little; we may have issues with self-control or want to control others. Some people work out these issues when training dogs, rationalizing that they're doing what's best for the pup. But are they?

Don't get me wrong: I believe that dogs need to be taught the family rules for their own safety and so that more of us keep them. It is the excessive, often ornamental training that attempts to alter the dog's essence solely to satisfy the owner's ego that I have problems with (I also have problems with the word "owner"). Training should be about making our dogs look good, not the other way around.

I remember listening to the lyrics of a song from *Guys and Dolls* as a child, "Marry the man today and change his ways tomorrow," and wondering, "Why?" Yet changing others, whether humans or animals, seems to be a fundamental need of many people. Of course, a dog's behaviors can be modified, enhanced, or toned down. But these behaviors are at the core of his being, the essence of who he is. Destroy that and he ceases to be.

There are those who believe that dogs are selfless souls who care only about pleasing their "master" (don't get me started on that word!). This is not only narcissistic but it is simply not so, and ultimately this belief does dogs a disservice. Here's what I mean: If dogs live to please us, then their chewing our shoe when we come home late seems proof positive of their spitefulness, right? Wrong. Dogs do what they do to meet *their* needs at that moment. They chew because they are teething, playing, bored, lonely, or scared. They seek out something of ours to chew to *connect* with us, not anger us. It soothes them; much like overeating soothes some of us.

Spitefulness sounds so sinister. It suggests an awareness of the past, present, and future in the creation of a diabolical plot: "Because you stayed out late last night, I'll chew your sneaker today so that you are on time tomorrow." It's way too complicated, and decidedly uncanine. Spite is a human contrivance. Yet, judging from how my clients react to this suggestion, it seems that humans are extremely invested in the notion of canine spite. What fuels this belief is the idea that a dog looks "guilty," as though he "had to know he shouldn't have chewed the sneaker." Wrong again. That guilty look is actually a mix of fear and confusion. He's discovered that you're mad at him when you come home, but he doesn't know why. Too much time has elapsed for him to connect your ire with his chewing (more on this in Chapter 2). I propose that whenever you start thinking your dog did something dastardly "to spite you," substitute "because he was stressed." Instead of, "Amelda chewed my shoe because I came home late last night *to spite me*," try, "because I came home late *Amelda was stressed* and therefore chewed my shoe." Either way it's bad news for the shoe, but hopefully you will be more compassionate if you understand the puppy's true motivation.

Dogs' biological clocks are accurate to within thirty seconds in a twenty-four-hour period. So although some routine is vital to a dog's training and security, too rigid a routine is a recipe for disaster. I will never forget the frantic phone call I got from Jennifer about her two Australian shepherds, Kanga and Roo. Jen followed an extremely regular routine. She always left the house at 6:45 A.M. to catch the train out of Westport, Connecticut, into New York City and always returned home at 7:15 P.M. Always. These dogs accepted being left for twelve and a half hours a day, five days a week. After ten months on this schedule, Jennifer missed the train and got home at 7:30 to discover the dogs had trashed the house. We're talking a shredded love seat, downed drapes, and a big old poop. That last fifteen minutes undid them. Their biological clocks were set for 7:15, and beyond that they could not cope. It is therefore vital to accustom dogs to exceptions to the rule by occasionally altering their routine.

We all have our own training objectives, so I won't presume to decide what's right for you. Instead I'd like to share my own training goals as a way of showing you what you can expect to accomplish with the information contained in this book. It is my goal to be able to include my dogs in whatever I'm doing without worry. I like taking them to friends' houses, the beach, New York City, the Memorial Day parade, B&Bs, and on car trips and long walks in the woods. I want my dogs with me while I garden and shovel snow. They should chew their things, not mine, leave me alone when I'm eating, come when called, poop outside, and be reliable on and off leash (though I would *never* walk any dog off lead near traffic). I'd appreciate their alerting me that a burglar is about and to then stop barking when I point out that it's just Mr. UPS. I expect them to be friendly to my guests without jumping all over them. But mostly, I just want my dogs to be happy, to love me, and to do what dogs do.

## CHAPTER 1

# The Right Dog for You

A client of mine with five children under the age of ten recently told me that her mild-mannered Newfoundland puppy was more work than her five kids. This blew my mind. She then explained that the babies wore diapers and never chewed furniture, and she didn't have to run home every few hours to check on them.

Dogs are too much work for too long and too expensive to maintain to be impulsively acquired. If you don't have time to think through getting a dog, you definitely don't have time to raise one. It offends me deeply that people go to the pet shop to buy fish food and come home with a puppy. Everything about pet shops' sale of dogs offends me, from the puppy mills where the puppies are bought, to the deplorable conditions on the trucks transporting them to the stores, to the sale of puppies to anyone off the street, no matter how impulsive or inappropriate their decision.

Of course there are exceptions; some pet shops are better than others, and many of these pups turn into wonderful adult dogs. Still, the latter experience is tantamount to driving drunk and *not* getting into an accident; it doesn't mean that it was a good idea in the first place. Most who buy a pet store puppy get saddled with an unhealthy animal who is difficult to housebreak and has significant behavioral problems. I once carried a placard in front of a pet shop that was being boycotted thanking the store. When a reporter asked me about this, I explained that I make a fortune working with these often-incorrigible dogs.

Pups that languish in pet stores too long get marked down, like last year's car model. A client told me recently that she "rescued" one such discounted dog for a mere $900, saying, "What a deal!" The corgi is psychotic. He spins in circles and attacks anyone who approaches

**13**

from his left side. Her rescued dog is immediately replaced by the store, thereby perpetuating an industry that we would be better off without.

If you plan on buying a pedigreed pup, research breed temperament and trainability and exercise and grooming requirements, as well as potential breed-specific medical and behavioral problems. No breed is perfect, so select one whose imperfections you can best live with. If you are very sensitive to sound, Shetland sheepdogs and schnauzers may be too vocal for you. The clean freak should steer clear of a big old hairy drooler like a Saint Bernard. Springer spaniels tend to be tireless and clumber spaniels are plodding. Labrador retrievers love everyone, while Chesapeake Bay retrievers are often reserved. Be realistic about your own energy level relative to Rover's. Do not pick a high-energy pup if you are not going to exercise him properly. Understimulation is a primary reason dogs get into trouble. Conversely, a dog who is sluggish may be overstimulated by too active a household and get grouchy. Make sure the breed's training requirements are consistent with your expectations. In general, a dog can handle as much training as he needs. Your easygoing Boston terrier pup may fade after five minutes, while an ambitious Border collie can work for hours—and needs to. Obvious though the above may seem, all too often people choose a breed based on looks alone.

Because dogs are individuals, there are plenty of exceptions to generalizations about each breed—and I caution against breed bigotry—but one of the advantages of pursuing a pedigreed pup is your ability to bone up on the breed's characteristics. Once you have done your research and chosen the breed that is right for you, look for a reputable breeder through personal and professional referrals and the Internet.

Some breeders unload mature dogs that are of no further use to them. One may fall short as a show dog, while another is too old or unproductive to continue breeding. If you are considering going this route, please be careful. Although many of these "breeder dogs" turn into terrific pets, in my experience most do not. A syndrome called "kennelosis" affects some dogs from large kennels, where they are viewed more as beasts of burden rather than potential companion animals. Like career criminals who cannot cope once paroled, these dogs can't function outside the kennel, the only home they know. Although a breeder dog may look beautiful, unless he is properly socialized and raised in a home, he may act more like a frilly farm animal than Lassie.

If you are thinking about adopting a dog through a shelter or pure breed rescue league, first check its reputation and then consider your own motivation. To adopt solely to save on the purchase price is a mistake. Recycled dogs often have medical or behavioral issues that will require professional intervention that costs more than you will save by adopting in the first place. People tend to assume that because a dog is mature he's housebroken. This isn't necessarily so. Besides, house-breaking, like toilet training, is only a big deal when you're in the thick of it. Chewing, barking, and escaping are far more difficult problems to live with, yet I've found that adoptive "parents" rarely think of these things, even though they may be why the dog was given up. It's true that a puppy does tend to tie you down more than a mature dog, but please don't make the mistake of thinking that integrating an adult dog into your life is effortless. Nothing worthwhile ever is.

Wherever you decide to get a dog, ask a lot of questions. When adopting a puppy, try to meet the mother, as her temperament will largely determine that of her brood. Insist upon seeing certificates from a veterinarian documenting that the puppy or his parents are free of breed-specific disorders and the vaccination history. Seven weeks is generally the ideal age to bring home a puppy behaviorally, but your hands may be tied here as breeders and shelters often have their own schedules.

The lengths some people go to in pursuit of the "perfect" puppy is something I will never understand. Those who believe such a puppy exists are destined for disappointment. It breaks my heart to hear of a puppy being shipped like cargo thousands of miles, sight unseen, simply because somebody has to have "the best." I also have to wonder what message that sends to the children in the family. I am currently working with "the best" six-month-old German shepherd, who was imported for $2,500. This handsome puppy's hips are already so horrific that he can't sit without whimpering.

People tell me all the time that their puppy picked them. I value this assessment as *part* of an informed decision. Sometimes, however, the pushiest pup climbs over his littermates, elbowing the littler ones out of the way to be the first to get to whoever is outside the whelping box. Beware, this bruiser may turn out to be a bully. I'd think twice about taking him home where there are young children or passive adults (more on bossy dogs on pages 96–99). I'd also discourage families with small children from selecting the shy puppy cowering in the corner.

**15**

He is a potential fear biter (see the Timid Dog section on pages 93–96). There is a trend for breeders to temperament test litters. These are tests used by breeders and in shelters to determine a puppy's or dog's dominance, trainability, responsiveness, and so forth. For example, rolling a puppy over to observe whether or not it struggles is alleged to be a test of dominance or submission. While I love the idea of testing a puppy's temperament and I'd take the results into consideration, I've not found such tests to be accurate often enough to be the deciding factor.

Because I believe in spaying and neutering all but the healthiest, best-tempered pedigreed puppies who will be responsibly bred, I wouldn't worry too much about whether you pick a boy or a girl. The difference in temperament between intact male and female dogs is diminished in those who are neutered. All things being equal, I would consider that dogs often bond better with people of the opposite sex. In the end, however, you should pick the puppy who most speaks to you.

Personally, I like adopting dogs in need of a home. I enjoy the challenge, get a kick out of the mystery of a multiple-pedigree dog, and feel good about saving a life. To date, I've lived with sixteen dogs. Eleven were puppies when I acquired them, five adults; six were pedigreed and ten were mutts. I have raised puppies from scratch who proved to be a handful as adults and adopted older dogs from the worst of circumstances who turned into the best pets.

Whether you acquire a puppy or a mature dog, a purebred or mixed breed, I applaud thoughtful decisions. Choosing to include a dog in your life may be one of the most important decisions you will ever make. Why shortchange yourself and the dog by making a shallow selection? To objectify a dog is to miss the point. Dogs are not about status or political correctness, they are about love. If one does not get this, one should not get a dog.

## Before You Bring a Puppy Home

Before you even bring little Rover home you need to equip yourself with the following basic supplies:

❏ Two stainless-steel or ceramic bowls

❏ Food (to begin stick with what he is already being fed)

❏ A crate

❏ Cozy bedding that's easy to wash

❏ Toys (try one squeaky, one bouncy, one fuzzy, one hard, one soft, and one chewable)

❏ Grooming supplies appropriate for the puppy's coat

❏ A soft little puppy collar and a lightweight cloth leash

❏ A chewing aversive (Bitter Apple is the product I recommend)

❏ A stain remover and odor neutralizer (Nature's Miracle is great for carpeting, and white vinegar works well on floors)

I also recommend researching veterinarians prior to acquiring Rover and taking the pup in for a checkup soon after bringing him home.

## Home Sweet Home: Crating

"Crate" is a euphemism for cage. Whatever you call it, I wouldn't raise a puppy without one. All pups need a cozy space of their own to be left in when no one's supervising. This obviously prevents their having access to things they shouldn't chew and it expedites housebreaking. It is natural for dogs to leave their living quarters to relieve themselves. Not wanting to soil the crate, most are highly motivated to hold on as long as they can.

Many people prefer to puppy-proof a laundry room or other small space, which is fine, but I prefer crates because they can be located where you are. If the crate is in the kitchen, den, or bedroom, the puppy can be included in the family's activities, which will ultimately make it easier to transition him into being in that room without a crate. Laundry rooms are typically cold, out-of-the-way spaces. Relegating Rover to one means you must make time to hang out with him there.

**CRATING MYTH #1: ALL DOGS LOVE THEIR CRATE.**

Many do, which is wonderful. Even more don't, which is fine, as long as they come to accept it. Rover doesn't have to love it to use it.

You should select a cage large enough for your dog to grow into, but if it's too big for the puppy, he may sleep in one end and relieve himself in the other, thereby defeating one of its purposes. This can be remedied by temporarily making the crate smaller by using a divider to cordon off part of it.

If floor space is limited, make a decorating statement by throwing a piece of fabric over the crate and calling it an end table. Have the kids draw pictures welcoming Rover home to hang outside the crate. The inside should be warm and homey, with washable bedding that smells like you and can be bunched up or pushed aside should the pup be warm and prefer to sleep on the bare floor. Don't situate the crate too close to a heating vent or in direct sunlight. And while it's great to have the cage near the action, make sure that it's not so central as to deny the pup quiet time. Think of it as his very own special space, complete with toys, treats, and housekeeping service. Your attitude about your puppy's crate will largely determine the ease with which he'll accept it.

When I first heard of crates twenty-odd years ago, I thought they were barbaric. Being a freedom freak, the thought of imprisoning my puppy went against everything I believed in. To this day I still place a premium on my animals' freedom. My adult dogs have unlimited access to the whole house; off-leash walks in the woods are my greatest joy; and my parrots, Murray and Uh-Oh, are only caged when home alone. Still, I have come to love crates.

Take your time acclimating Rover to his cage. Tedious though this is, it's your ticket to training success. Have the crate set up and equipped with bedding, toys, and treats when you bring the puppy home. If he walks into it on his own, tell him what a good boy he is. Exiting should go unacknowledged. Feed him at least his first few meals in there. It is completely kosher to toss a treat into the crate to encourage him. When entering it is no big deal, close the door while you stay in the room. Mild protestations are to be expected. Simply ignore these, wait for

Rover to settle down, if only briefly, and then nonchalantly let him out. You want to downplay his departure from the crate.

Should the puppy be reluctant to enter the crate on his own after a few days, try a little reverse doggy psychology: Put all sorts of really cool stuff in it—primo toys, gourmet goodies, T-Bills—and lock him *out*. I did this with my puppy Buddha. In six minutes flat she was pleading with me to *please, please, please* let her in.

Once Rover tolerates brief crate enclosures with you in the room, slowly extend the time you leave him there while you go about your business. Hand him something to chew before confining him. Your goal is to push him to twenty minutes before letting him out. This may take a few trials.

When the puppy tolerates a twenty-minute stretch in the crate, it's time to crate him and leave the room but stay in the house. Unless he is in serious danger of hurting himself, it is essential that you ignore all protestations. Negotiating with him runs the risk of encouraging the very behaviors you want to end. The puppy will interpret your "there, there" as praise for acting out. Scolding him may make matters even worse. Counterintuitive though it seems, correcting Rover at this point may condition him to be really obnoxious to get a rise out of you. If you ignore quiet whimpering but then cave when he begins to bark, for example, clever Rover quickly figures out that barking brings you back. This will become his entry-level complaint next time around. Even yelling "Shut up!!" may be better than no attention at all. The opposite of positive reinforcement is not negative reinforcement; it is indifference.

## CRATING MYTH #2: A DOG WILL NEVER SOIL HIS CRATE.

Although most dogs are highly motivated to keep their cages clean, if a dog is sick or left too long, he's gonna go. I recently spoke with an irate woman whose nine-week-old bichon frise peed and pooped in the crate he was left in for eight hours. "I was told a dog would never mess in his cage," she complained. "I'd have had an accident too," I explained, "if I couldn't make it to the john all day. And I'm housebroken."

That is why ignoring him is the only way to succeed. The puppy's carrying on will cease so long as you don't fuel it. This, of course, is equally applicable to other situations in which Rover doth protest.

And now the pièce de résistance: It is time to leave crated Rover home alone. Arrange to do this when he has been well exercised, is not hungry, and has recently relieved himself. Once he has been settled in the crate for about twenty minutes, say "Ciao" and calmly leave the house. After about twenty minutes—the minimum time it seems to take for new behaviors to become established—return equally calmly and take him outside. From here, slowly build up his tolerance for being left home alone.

The speed with which a puppy becomes acclimated to his crate varies significantly. Most accept the crate in about five days. This entire process may even be unnecessary for the puppy who has been successfully crate conditioned by the breeder.

> Be aware that there are some puppies who panic when confined. This is rare, but confining such a dog with severe separation anxiety or one who was previously traumatized in a crate may be too dangerous. I have heard of desperate pups getting their feet or jaws stuck, and in one case of a dog dying from injuries incurred while trying to escape. How to manage such a dog will also be addressed in the Lonely Dog section (pages 99–104).

Pet shop puppies are often forced to relieve themselves in their cages, either in the store or at the puppy mills from which they came. The same can be true for pups from some shelters. Having been raised in filth, many lose their motivation to stay clean. A puppy in this situation will get covered in his own excrement when crated, and cleaning him and the cage is a chore. These dogs and those who panic in the crate are best confined to a small room with a gate.

Once acclimated, young Rover can be left in the crate or small space when no one is supervising. Like a playpen, it should be a happy space and not used punitively. How many hours to confine him at a clip is contingent upon his age, activity level, and biological needs. This will be discussed further in the Housebreaking section (pages 38–42).

How long to use a crate is largely a lifestyle decision. Some people crate their dogs for life. Others keep the crate but reduce their dog's reliance on it by using it only occasionally. Personally, because I live in a small house with big dogs, I'm always eager to reclaim the real estate occupied by a crate once my puppy is housebroken and no longer a chewing liability. However, I wouldn't get rid of the crate before the puppy is ten months old, as there is often a chewing regression around that age. Moving around the house has got to be more comfortable and interesting for them, and when they are free they are better able to scare away prowlers and wayward evangelists.

In general, one year is a pretty safe age to wean Rover from his crate if you decide to go that route. Take your time here. Let's say the cage is in the kitchen. Puppy-proof the room as best you can, then, when you're ready to go out briefly at a time when Rover's tired, go through the usual drill: Toss a treat into the cage, hand him a toy, and leave, but oops! *Forget* to fully close the crate door. The point of this ruse is to convey nonchalance. Rover can also pretend he didn't notice the open door should he not be ready to brave it alone. I knew a shy dog, Nola, who chose not to notice for months. The chew toy you handed to the dog just before leaving will be freshly scented with Eau de Tu, so that he will (hopefully) seek it out to chew in a moment of weakness. Calmly return within twenty minutes and go about your normal routine. If the TV or radio is usually on in that room, leaving it on may be soothing. However, turning it on only when you leave will signal your departure and make matters worse. Some mild acting out is to be expected at first, such as whining or pawing at the door. Simply ignore this. Allow two weeks to slowly transition Rover out of the crate, and keep it around for a few more weeks in case there are setbacks.

## CHAPTER 2

# Getting Ready to Teach the Basics

Understanding the appropriate use of reinforcement, voice tone, timing, clickers, and other concepts discussed in this chapter is essential to teaching Rover his ABCs.

## Hand Signals

'm big on hand signals. Learning a visual cue in addition to a verbal one is like learning both French and Spanish. Hand signals also encourage Rover's watchfulness and make him more inclined to look to you for guidance. This is especially valuable if your dog loses his hearing, as often happens in old age. Hand signals provide consistent communication, thereby minimizing the disorientation of deafness. Old Rover can no longer hear a car coming, but he can see your hand telling him to STAY out of the driveway. He doesn't know you are calling him, but he will recognize your signal to COME.

## Food Rewards

When I got started in this field twenty-three years ago, the use of food as a reward was frowned upon. "Bribery," we called it. Because we thought that dogs lived to please us, a simple "good dog" was more than enough. Today some trainers still adhere to this old belief, but it seems that even more now believe that the only way to teach a dog to do *anything* is with food. As my waistline will attest, moderation with food is not my strong suit. However, in dog training, I believe it is the way to go.

Food is the preferred currency of most dogs, but it is by no means the only one for which they will work. There are some dogs I call "ball savants," for whom a tennis ball is as good as it gets. Take advantage of naturally occurring reinforcers, like water for a thirsty dog or exercise for one who's pent up. I also believe that touch and voice tone are greatly underutilized training tools. I am certain that my talking to dogs is a big part of my success.

**25**

And although I applaud most modern dog trainers for preferring food to abuse, these aren't the only two options. Learning to use one's voice and hands effectively admittedly takes finesse and a certain amount of artistry, but for me, this is where the magic lies. Dogs are very sensual beings. Touching and talking to them can be both stimulating and soothing, and they are invaluable tools in the bonding process. Yes, dogs love food, but to use it exclusively limits the extent to which we can communicate with them. Viewing their behavior simply as nothing more than a conditioned response is tantamount to reducing them to rats in a maze. Dogs are complex creatures with hearts and souls. And mine have a sense of humor. I encourage you to honor Rover's spirit as well as his palate. To do less is to miss the full picture.

Don't get me wrong; I use a lot of food in training. The point is that it is not the only tool that I use. Food is a great way to break the ice with timid dogs, and it is essential in teaching dogs to COME. I think it is sensible to toss a treat in a crate to encourage a puppy to enter it. I insist my own dogs earn all treats, yet they don't get one for every good thing they do.

I actually prefer to feed my dogs smaller meals and have them work for the rest of their rations, as wild canids would have to. If dogs can get something for free, why should they work for it? If I got paid whether or not I showed up for work, you'd best believe I'd take the day off.

When using food as canine currency, I put different values on treats and dole out the good stuff sparingly. Although a boring old biscuit may be enough to motivate a pooped puppy to sit, it may take a piece of chicken to get him to COME to you in the dog park.

When teaching a new behavior, it's reasonable to reward Rover every time he does it. Once the behavior is learned, however, begin to reduce the use of the reinforcer before the pup becomes too reliant on it. The intentional withholding of rewards actually allows you to strengthen behaviors by selecting only his best efforts to reinforce. So if it had taken four requests for Rover to begrudgingly COME when called, now only reward him when he comes more quickly and with less attitude. Where treats were once his paycheck, they're now a bonus, and he has to work extra hard to earn one. This way, you won't need to worry about Rover being unwilling to COME if you forget to bring treats to the park. He will already be conditioned to come for free occasionally. Nothing untrains someone faster than denying him a perceived entitlement.

## Practicing

When it comes to practicing, please *don't,* at least not in an obvious way. What's more boring than to drill a dog to sit, sit, and sit again in the den for half an hour after dinner? I'd prefer you find ways to incorporate Rover's training into actual activities throughout the day: SIT before meals and treats; STAY at the door and to have the ball thrown; lie DOWN while you have dinner or watch TV.

## "Look at Me"

"Look at me" is an eminently useful little exercise. From day one, encourage Rover to check in by tweaking your fingers in front of your eyes while sweetly saying his name and then, "look at me." Smile to ensure soft eyes. If added incentive is needed in the beginning, move a choice toy or treat from his nose to your eyes to encourage him to "look." Think of "look at me" as a preamble to training. "Rover, look at me, good boy!" Now ask him to SIT or LIE DOWN or whatever. Our goal is for Rover to ultimately look at you for direction without your even asking.

"Look at me" is also an effective way to preempt unwanted behaviors by getting Rover's attention in advance of his acting out. Being unable to multitask, if Rover is looking at you he can't also snarl at the mailman, chase a rabbit, or bark at a basenji.

This is a relationship-building exercise. Never ask Rover to LOOK and then scowl or try to stare him down (something I never recommend anyway). "Look at me" is a matter of trust. If you abuse it you will lose it.

## Voice Commands

Some people get all caught up in the choice of words they use to train their dogs. They worry whether to say "drop" or "release," "look" or "watch," "down" or "off." Remember that they're dogs, not William Safire: The subtleties of the English language are wasted on them. In Tokyo, dogs can even learn where to pee in Japanese. I was once hired by a woman to train her husband's German short-haired pointer, Wolfgang, to do the wrong tricks as a practical joke. When the husband ordered Wolfgang to "speak," the dog played dead; he'd say "shake,"

27

and Wolfgang barked. For further proof that the words don't matter, try the following: In your sweetest, most lovey-dovey voice tell Rover "you are the dumbest dog in the whole wide world." Ten to one, he'll lay a wet juicy one on you and say, "Thank you very much."

### JUST SAY NO!

Many trainers recommend using a different word to correct each of Rover's transgressions. Though there's nothing wrong with this method, I prefer to use a simple "No!" Whether the pup is chewing the carpet, rummaging through the garbage, or running toward the road, I want him to stop the moment he hears the word. Proponents of a more varied lexicon contend that overuse of this word or any other dilutes its potency. I agree, but if you find yourself overusing the word, you should consider why the poor puppy is being told "no" so often anyway. The whole point of training is to teach Rover what he should do, so that reacting to what he should not do is kept to a minimum.

### VOICE

Varying your voice tone and volume is an invaluable teaching tool. Use a soft, natural voice to ask things of Rover. He can hear a Frito fall at 250 yards; there's no need to yell. Besides, here's where you literally set the tone of his training. Do you want to be heard screaming COME forever? Praise your dog in a singsongy voice at a higher pitch than normal. Bark "No!" just once, so that he can associate it with what's unacceptable, then immediately redirect Rover in your nice, soft voice to the original request. Sound lively to motivate active exercises like HEEL, and unemotional to suggest STAY.

## Clickers

Clickers—small, inexpensive plastic and metal boxes that, when compressed, make a clicking sound—are all the rage in dog training these days. There are clicker books and videos, workshops, and a newsletter. They're being used with dogs and cats, with horses and llamas, and in zoos and circuses.

Clickers have been around since the 1940s, but they were popularized in the 1990s by dolphin trainer and behaviorist Karen Pryor, whose wonderful book with a terrible title, *Don't Shoot the Dog,* is a behaviorist bible. Some trainers use clickers to teach everything, and others find them too newfangled to bother with. I fall somewhere in between.

Clickers are primarily used in dog training as *conditioned reinforcers,* but they can also be used as *conditioned stimuli* (more on these below). The click itself is not what matters. Rather, it is a neutral sound that is made meaningful when associated with something great. It's important that the sound precede the treat, as it is meant to foretell good things.

Dr. Ivan Pavlov's experiments taught us with those drooling dogs how *conditioned stimuli* affect involuntary behavior. As you probably know, Pavlov rang a bell (actually a metronome), then offered the dogs meat (which was really just meat powder), and they salivated while eating the meat. Bell, meat, drool. Bell, meat, drool. After a number of repetitions, the dogs began to drool upon hearing the bell in anticipation of the meat. In short order, Pavlov was able to eliminate the middleman—the meat—and still elicit the same amount of dribble using the metronome alone. Bell, drool. Bell, drool. When the neutral sound was paired with food, it became every bit as compelling as the meat itself. If A=B and B=C, then A=C (ish).

If you would rather teach your dog to listen than to drool, you can use the sound of the clicker as a *conditioned reinforcer. Unconditioned* reinforcement, like food, toys, and touch, is good all by itself, but conditioned reinforcement is symbolic. For example, for my birthday I was given a gift certificate to a day spa. The certificate, though only paper, made me happy because it meant I could get a massage. I was *conditioned* to respond to the certificate, whereas the massage was *unconditionally* delicious.

Dolphin trainers traditionally use whistles as conditioned reinforcers because the sound travels underwater. Let's say you're trying to teach your dolphin to jump. First, you establish the conditioned reinforcer by blowing the whistle then tossing Flipper a fish. Whistle, fish. Whistle, fish. The whistle means a mackerel is imminent. Now when Flipper jumps spectacularly the whistle alone will say "Good dolphin."

Dog trainers prefer clickers to whistles because they leave our mouths free, as we're a chatty lot. But before you use the clicker as a training tool, like the whistle, it needs to be primed so that Rover understands that it is a good thing. If we wanted to, we could just as easily prime it to be a bad thing. But let's don't.

Loud enough to be heard outdoors, the click can be startling inside, so muffle the noise by holding the clicker in your pocket or behind your back. Click just once and then give Rover a treat. He doesn't have to earn it yet. Click and treat. As you're going to be doing this many times, use small treats. The click always comes first. Click then treat. Keep doing this until the sound alone excites the pup. This usually only takes a few minutes. Vary the lag time between the click and the treat. We want him to know that he may have to wait but that he will eventually get the goods. Occasionally withhold the food altogether, since it is our ultimate goal to only need to reinforce Rover intermittently with treats.

The clicker becomes another way to praise; I therefore click at the same time I say "Good boy." Why do we need another way to praise? Good question. With the clicker everyone in the household can praise the dog identically without worrying about their tone of voice, posture, or hand position. When I first learned about clickers I was hired by Boris, an Eastern European man with a deep, gravelly voice whose "Good boy, Marx" terrified his poor cocker spaniel. Unable to soften his voice enough, Boris clicked to say "Good boy."

The brevity of the click can also isolate an element out of a series of behaviors that you want to reinforce. So if Rover enthusiastically COMES when called, you can quickly click to reward his arrival just before he plows into you.

There are two mistakes you can make with the clicker:

1. **Clicking too close to the puppy's ear and scaring him.** Never click closer than three feet away from your puppy, as this may permanently turn him off of the clicker. If the clicker frightens him for this or any reason, don't use it.

2. **Clicking when he's misbehaving.** This will simply reinforce the undesired behavior.

**30**

The clicker is not for everyone. Coordinating its use can be a little like patting your head while rubbing your belly, but you needn't worry about the details as long as you avoid the two mistakes mentioned above. Clickers are primarily used when teaching something new. Once the lesson is mastered and Rover has proven his reliability for six weeks, always having a clicker around is not practical. It's time to slowly phase out using it over a two-week period. I resisted clickers at first, but for reasons I still don't fully understand, clickers can bring about such dramatic results that I have become a convert.

## Timing

Timing is tricky. Dogs live in the here and now. The last thing your dog did is what he thinks you're acknowledging, so you must respond *immediately* to the action you intend to address. I call this the Zen of dog training. Reacting too early or too late reinforces the wrong behavior, the behavior that is occurring at precisely *that* moment. For example, recently I worked with Tempo, a five-month-old bearded collie whose jumping is driving his person crazy. During our session Tempo pooped outside, where he was supposed to, and then jumped on Hedi while she lavished praise on him. She, of course, meant to reinforce his housebreaking, but instead she rewarded the jumping. It was what the dog was doing. This works in reverse, too. Let's say Hedi was still scolding Tempo's jumping while he squatted to pee. What message would that send? Ill-timed feedback is at the core of scores of training troubles.

The one characteristic shared by the best trainers—and comedians—is great timing. We need to consider timing not only when giving feedback, but also when deciding when to cue a desired behavior. Here, we tend to do things backwards. Don't decide it's time to teach Tempo to COME when he's running away from you in hot pursuit of a squirrel. If, day after day, this is the only time he hears COME, how is Tempo to know that it means anything other than "run after a rodent"? It's like saying "down" whenever the baby points up.

## Aversives

There is no more controversial topic in dog training than the use of aversives. An aversive is anything that Rover strongly dislikes. It could be a taste, smell, sound, or sensation. There are aversive trainers whose first course of action is to use an aversive in hopes of forcing Rover to make the right choice to avoid the discomfort. I don't even want to dignify this approach. Then there are those who believe that it is morally reprehensible to ever use even the mildest of aversives. I don't believe this is the best approach either, but at least this is erring in the right direction.

Dog owners' beliefs can be equally extreme. I was hired by a man whose Italian greyhound, Luigi, had chewed an electrical cord, the passenger seat of an SUV, and the corner of an antique armoire in a week. Luigi was pampered to the point of pathology. My client held him on his lap the entire hour and a half I was there and didn't seem to notice Luigi's nonstop mouthing of his hand. One of my many recommendations was using an aversive spray on the furniture to curb Luigi's excessive chewing. The man's "How could you?" expression demonstrated the depth to which this suggestion offended him. Yet the house was filled with his hunting trophies. Conversely, I am currently working with a disheveled woman who appears totally out of control of her own life but is furious with me for refusing to use a shock collar to housebreak her Welsh terrier.

> **In light of such extreme and divergent views, I want to clarify my position on aversive usage. I will only use an aversive if I cannot get the desired result by first using positive training. If I deem an aversive to be necessary, I will always use the mildest one that works and for the briefest period possible. The only time I would use an aversive that causes pain is if Rover or his person's safety would be jeopardized without it. I will immediately follow aversive usage with a review of what Rover should have done, and end on a positive note.**

The purpose of an aversive is to quickly interrupt an undesirable behavior so that you can work on what is acceptable. To correct without redirecting your dog's behavior is a missed opportunity, an incomplete thought. Aversives do not teach a thing. You do.

## CHAPTER 3

# Puppy Stuff

The most un-fun part of puppy rearing is dealing with chewing, mouthing, and houscbreaking. As thankless as the process feels, I promise that you'll be ever so thankful once it's past.

## Chewing

Puppies chew. It's what they do. Some are specialists; stuffed animals are their thing. Then you've got your generalists—they'll chew the hard, soft, fuzzy, or fringed—the equal opportunity chewer.

Common items puppies like to chew are: shoes, corners of kitchen cabinets, throw rugs, their leash, and Legos. They'll chew almost anything that smells like you: hats, gloves, engagement rings, toupees, retainers, underpants, Band-Aids, bracelets, hair scrunchies, scarves, pantyhose, hearing aids, socks, tampons, eyeglasses, hands, and brassieres. And there's the remote control, sponge, Beanie Baby, towel, seat belt, pillow, pencil, teddy bear, lipstick, place mat, dental floss, magazine, banister, shoelace, cardboard, pot holder, coaster, in-law, bedspread, crayon, fringe, wallpaper, sofa, cookbook, cat poop, emery board, diaper, newspaper, telephone, mouse pad, mouse, paper towel, disposable razor, pencil, napkin, and backpack chewer.

They really love to chew.

The issue, then, isn't *whether* he will chew, but *what* he will chew. Your job is to set up his environment from day one so that the right chewing choices are obvious. "His environment" could mean the kitchen, the yard, or wherever the puppy is allowed to play while being supervised. Since some puppies will chew doorjambs, molding, and trees, it's impossible to puppy-proof an area 100 percent. Spraying a chewing aversive like Bitter Apple, a nontoxic, nonstaining product whose taste most dogs dislike, on what's verboten from the beginning will make such a powerful impression on your puppy that he won't ever chew that item. By leaving a toy next to what's off limits, the environ-

35

ment showed him what to and not to chew. *Don't* chew the sofa; *do* chew the rubber ducky. *Don't* chew my sock; *do* chew your bone. (More on this in the Entrapment section on pages 84–87.)

To avoid having to live in a house perfumed with Bitter Apple, try pairing the aversive scent with another aroma you like. Gradually discontinue using the unpleasant odor while still spraying the fragrant one. Many dogs will have made the olfactory association and will continue to avoid the sweet-smelling stuff. You are left with an aromatic, intact house. If Rover's an avid hand or clothing nosher, using your perfume here will teach him not to chew you.

> **A note on Bitter Apple: There are some little stinkers out there that actually like the taste of Bitter Apple. This, of course, defeats its purpose. If your puppy likes it, either try other commercially prepared products or improvise with lemon juice, Tabasco sauce, or Listerine sprayed from a plant mister.**

Obvious though it sounds, always make a big deal out of the pup's chewing his own toys. In my experience, people tend to take this for granted. And, although it is important that Rover is well equipped with toys, covering the floor with wall-to-wall toys may make it difficult for him to discriminate between the items on the floor that are his and those that are not. (It used to be that a knotted sock or an old tennis ball was all Rover could hope for. Now there are educational dog toys, Santa Fe Chicken Cornstarch bones, toys that walk and talk, and some that even glow in the dark.) Six toys at a time, which can be rotated, should be plenty.

### TEETHING

Puppies are born toothless, but their needle-sharp little "milk teeth" soon start to grow in, and then begin to fall out at around four months. Between four and six months they get all of their adult teeth. If humans teethed at such a rate, we'd chew an Audi.

That stretch between four and six months is tough. Rover is miserable. Give him an occasional ice cube or frozen carrot, or try the following: Soak dried dog food in chicken broth until it becomes mushy. Stuff it into a Kong (a hard rubber dog toy) or a hollowed out marrow bone (not to worry, pet shops sell the cleaned bones), then throw it in the freezer. Adding a little peanut butter, chicken, or cheese will make it extra scrumptious. You might as well make up a few while you're at it. Depending upon the size of the puppy, either eliminate one meal or reduce its quantity and instead hand the pup a frozen bone. This will keep him contentedly chewing while numbing his sore gums. The Kong has the added advantage of bouncing.

File the following under "Do as I say, not as I do." I probably shouldn't even tell you. A wolf biologist friend sent me a lichen-covered musk ox vertebra from the Arctic Circle that had been perfectly preserved in the permafrost. It was believed to be about 750 years old. Quite the treasure. My puppy Stinky thought so too. With items of irreplaceable value, don't tempt fate. A bone is a bone is a bone. It is inevitable that your puppy's chewing will destroy something. I have never known otherwise. You might as well anticipate this, minimize your losses, and move on.

### MOUTHING

Mouthing means chewing on you. It is something all puppies do, although there are many professionals—vets, breeders, groomers, and trainers—who will tell you that all mouthing is a capital offense, a precursor to biting, and must be stopped tout de suite. I disagree. And talk about setting yourself up to fail! Being unable to send flowers, hug, or flip someone the bird, your puppy expresses himself by mouthing. Only in the context of mouthing can he be taught to be gentle and to ultimately inhibit his bite.

Your hands are food givers, lifters, and training tools. They are not chew toys. To wave them seductively in a puppy's face is an absolute invitation for him to bite them. It's like handing your child a cupcake and then scolding her for eating it. So don't do it. A pup is less inclined to mouth on a hand reaching *under* than *over* his head. When Rover softly mouths or licks your hand, say "gentle" or "kisses" in a gooey voice. If his mouthing hurts—and with those little needle-sharp teeth that's not unlikely—let your hand go limp. For many puppies, deactivating your hand makes it unfun. If this isn't enough, yip "ouch" like a wounded puppy. Immediately redirect him to be "gentle" or give

**37**

"kisses," or offer him a chew toy. Make the chew toy extra attractive by rubbing it, thereby seasoning it with your flavor. Reluctant Rover may become interested in the toy if you first squeak it, bounce it, or play hard to get with it before finally letting him have it. I typically say, "This is what a good dog chews." In time, saying "kisses," "gentle," or "What's a good dog chew?" will be all you need to prompt those behaviors.

Dogs are most likely to mouth you when you're sitting on the floor with them. Being on the floor makes us doglike, and there is nothing dogs like more than mouthing. If you're on the ground and Rover's mouthing gets too intense, simply stand up. Being bigger is often enough to change the dynamic. Think of sitting on the floor as a privilege for the puppy, one that's denied when he gets too rough.

Some children have a hard time with this. We adults were only on the floor because of the puppy, but kids consider it their own domain, and being asked to share their turf could cause resentment. Typically, if the puppy's mouthing is annoying enough, children are willing to relinquish the floor. And for the puppy whose mouthing overwhelms young children, spraying a little Bitter Apple on the kid's clothing should do the trick. Providing both the children and the puppy with their own really cool play stations may help to ease this type of sibling rivalry.

## The Inside Poop: Housebreaking

Nothing brings a grown man to his knees more quickly than ill-placed poop. You'd think it was plutonium. Many women are no better. Euphemisms abound: A neurosurgeon referred to his dog "making number 2," and a senior vice president of a Fortune 500 company called it a "Tootsie Roll." I assure you, but for the stray stick, a puppy's waste is no more hazardous than your own. Get a grip! Besides, it's the pee that will come back to haunt you.

**38**   *FROM ADOPTION TO THREE MONTHS OLD*

Puppies at this age have no real sphincter muscle control, so this is your pre-training month. Hang a bell on the inside handle of the exit door and make a point of ringing it every time you take him out. Go outdoors with the puppy as often as you can and praise him for relieving himself there in order to show him the final goal. As the pup squats say something like "Hurry up," "Get busy," "Go potty," "Richard Nixon," or whatever. Observe what he does right before relieving himself. Does he circle, dig, sniff, whine, or kink his tail? Our goal for this month is to get lucky as often as possible in order to maximize opportunities to praise the puppy for pooping and peeing outdoors and to minimize cleaning up inside.

Let's say the crate is in the kitchen and that's the puppy's designated domain for now. He should be offered food and water in the crate for the first week and only closed in for brief periods of time. Young puppies are peeing machines. Closing him in the crate for long stretches now will force him to pee in there, which undermines the ultimate goal of his leaving it to relieve himself. At this stage, simply ignore his going inside and clean thoroughly with an odor neutralizer.

Some people opt to permanently paper train their small dogs. This may be appropriate in cities, or for the elderly, shut-in, or lazy. Active paper training involves taking the pup to the paper when you suspect he needs to go and praising him for doing so. For the rest of us, to purposefully paper train doubles the work, as you'll soon have to teach him *not* to use it. Passive paper training involves strategically placing paper about in hopes that he'll hit it, thereby making cleanup easier. The difference is that this goes unacknowledged. Taking soiled papers outdoors may provide a helpful hint for puppies who have a hard time with this transition.

Where the puppy sleeps at night is a lifestyle decision. My own dogs have always slept in my bedroom. It's our bonus bonding time. All I have to do is sleep and they get to hear, see, and smell me. I understand that this may not be what you want, but if it is, you might as well bite the bullet and do so from day one. Those first few nights can be tough. The poor thing just left his family of origin and doesn't know where anything is yet. Chances are, however, that he'll sleep more soundly in the bedroom with you than alone in the kitchen. At this age, Rover will probably need to relieve himself during the night. If getting up in the middle of the night to take him outside is too painful to bare, simply leave the crate door open so he can exit it to go on paper. Protect carpeting by cordoning off an area with gates or an Exercise-Pen and use a piece of linoleum to define the space.

## ABOUT THE BELL

People often ask me how to teach their dogs to bark when they need to go out. You don't. To reward barking with an outing runs the risk of creating a barking problem: "Woof! I wanna chase the squirrel." "Woof, woof! Here comes that foxy beagle!" "Woof, woof, woof! Mr. Mailman, watch out!" (More on this in the Nuisance Barking and Bossy Dog sections, pages 81–84 and 96–99.) Stopping problem barking is harder than housebreaking.

In as few as five days, most dogs come to associate the bell's ringing with the door opening and can ring it themselves to ask to go out. You can hasten his catching on by taking his little nose or paw and gently showing him how to ring it. Look for decorative bells or wind chimes that hang so that the pup can easily reach them. Should Rover develop the rare but ever-so-annoying bell-ringing habit, simply remove the bell. No further undoing need be done.

### THREE TO FOUR MONTHS OLD

Now we're getting serious. First thing in the morning take the puppy out. Generalize the toileting terrain by taking him to the same area, whether that be the periphery, pachysandra, wood chips, etc. I don't believe in being *too* specific though, lest you teach the pup that this is the only place you ever want him to go. Be flexible: If you're intent on his using the northwest corner of the yard and he's attracted to the southeast, so long as it's not in the middle of your perennial garden, I'd be happy he's learned to discriminate; not all dogs do and end up going anywhere and everywhere despite your best efforts. Unless you have a lot of acreage, you'll need to periodically scoop the poop wherever he goes. If it piles up, Rover will choose another, tidier toilet. As the puppy begins to sniff or circle in the way you've observed means that he's about to relieve himself, drone "Hurry up," wait until he's finished, and cheer "Good boy!" These words are an optional way of suggesting to the puppy what he's there to do. This will be very helpful if you travel with the pup and when you're in a rush. Many puppies squat a number of times on that first outing. Once he has finished relieving himself, play outside with him for a few minutes. To rush young Rover straight in may teach him to delay doing anything to stay outside longer.

Now it's time for Rover's breakfast. I believe in feeding a natural diet including wholesome fresh foods and unlimited drinking water. You may have been told that limiting the water will help with housebreaking. I hate this. Would you deny your child fluids to hasten toilet training? Dogs only drink as much water as they need to be healthy. Besides, restricting water may backfire by encouraging your dog to go into camel mode and drink excessively when he has the chance.

Feed him three meals a day when he is at this age: first thing in the morning, at midday, and in the late afternoon. By day, the three- to four-month-old puppy will probably poop four times and need to pee every few hours. Take him out presumptively upon awakening, when the kids come home, after his meals and rough play, and when he laughs. Otherwise, listen for the bell and look for that specific sniffing or circling signal and rush him outside. Overnight, everything slows down. By four months he *may* even make it through the night. Dare to dream.

The key to housebreaking is supervision. Given the immediacy with which dogs learn what is and is not acceptable, you can only respond appropriately if you see what he's doing. The puppy will assume everything's copacetic unless told otherwise. To allow lone Rover to roam into the guestroom and take a dump means—doggy de facto—it's okay. He is *outside* the kitchen, after all, and no one said boo when he did it. We think of outside as being where the deer and antelope play. To him, it's anywhere other than where he's confined. The less lived in the space, the better. So while containment is an essential part of supervision, intentionally introducing the puppy to the house is another. Having too much of the house be off-limits for too long runs the risk of your mature dog making this mistake upon his first sallying forth. From the beginning, therefore, take your puppy into every room he will eventually have access to. Do so when he has recently relieved himself, chew toy in tow, one room at a time, and allow him to investigate for ten to fifteen minutes. It wouldn't hurt to bring something to clean up with, just in case.

The primary benefit of such strict surveillance is being able to intervene if the puppy has an accident. Simply interrupt him by saying

"No!" and rush him outdoors to finish. Pick up the poop and take it out with you by way of showing him where to do his "Richard Nixons." The redirecting of accidents is important. It's easy to get lazy here; after all, the pup's already gone, it's raining, and you've got cramps. Don't yell when you catch him; this might inadvertently teach him to be sneaky. I learned this lesson with my puppy Plain Jane twenty-one years ago when my then-husband Marc screamed at her for pooping on the rug. Because he didn't promptly redirect her outside, P. J. had no way of knowing that her mistake was one of location. Instead, she simply thought she wasn't supposed to poop in front of him. So she didn't. This made Marc's walking her in New York City a challenge. More often than not, P. J. would hold on until she could get away from him inside and unload behind the potted plants. The goal is to emphasize praise for the right choices and to downplay corrections.

Another don't: Don't rub your dog's nose in his excrement. Yuck! The only aversive aspect to it is your wrath. Dogs adore the smell of pee and poop. Who makes this stuff up anyway?

When supervision is not possible, crate him. At this age he should be able to handle confinement by day for two to three hours at a clip. Our goal is for Rover to be at least 80 percent housebroken by four months.

### FOUR TO SIX MONTHS AND BEYOND

Now that the basic concepts of housebreaking have been taught, the next two months are about incrementally increasing the time between trips out. Rover needs to learn that there is a reliable rhythm to the day. By six months, he should need to go out every four to five hours by day and every seven to eight hours at night.

Warning: Puppies don't know from weekends, so forget about sleeping in for a while. And as with all learning, there will be advances and regressions. Bad weather, illness, and change in diet or routine may make him slip up. Not to worry: This is totally natural and no cause for concern.

After the puppy passes the six-month mark you might be able to eke out an extra hour or so between outings. Dogs all over are locked indoors all day while their people work, and many do remarkably well. Still, I can't bear the thought of this, and I encourage you to find a way for him to get a midday tinkle break.

## CHAPTER 4

# The ABCs of Training

All dogs need to learn the basics. Begin at the beginning with SIT, STAY, DOWN, COME, and HEEL. Training your dog to respond to basic commands will make your life together easier, safer, and provide a solid foundation for more advanced training. **43**

**Sit happens.**

SIT, STAY, DOWN, COME, and HEEL are the basic obedience exercises all dogs need to learn. Teaching your puppy these commands is as fundamental as teaching your child the three R's. They are the stepping-stones on the way to advanced training and problem solving. You can begin teaching baby Rover SIT and COME in brief, jolly snippets from day one. A minute or two here and there is enough. As he becomes more attentive, typically between three and four months, gently introduce STAY, DOWN, and HEEL. Between four and six months, most puppies are mature enough to pursue the following program fully.

### Sit

SIT is the simplest and most useful exercise of all. Think of SIT as meaning "I'm in control." When in doubt, ask Rover to SIT.

To teach SIT, stand close to Rover and scoop your hand up and over his head in a semicircle, starting at chest level and arching toward his rear end. Wiggle your fingers to engage his eyes. As your dog's head moves up and back to follow your hand, his tush will go down, and, voilà, SIT happens. Once he is in position, tell him what a good boy he is while petting his chest. Now it's time for a treat. And give Rover one, too.

The hand signal can be minimized in time, but when learning something new, its elements are often exaggerated. Remember learning to drive? We spent ten minutes adjusting the seat belt and getting the rearview mirror just right. And forget about parallel parking. Now we just get in the car and drive.

**45**

The time to say SIT is as he moves into position. The operative words here are "*he* moves." Forcing him will only cause him to resist. The most you can hope for by pushing Rover's rear end down when saying SIT is to condition him to tolerate coercion. Instead you want to facilitate the pup's figuring out how to do it himself. Humans generally want to learn in the same way. For example, I play drums. When, with creative coaching, I decipher a complex rhythm, it is such a rush that I retain the progression in a way I wouldn't have had my teacher placed my hands into position. I own it. So it is for Rover.

Once the association is made between the action and the word, saying SIT will prompt him to do so. Rover will learn that sitting is a prelude to good things: Food, thrown balls, and walks may follow. While he has to SIT to make good things happen, they don't automatically happen *every* time he sits. And because SIT means "I'm in control," redirect Rover to SIT whenever you're feeling out of control.

---

### SIT TROUBLE-SHOOTING TIPS

Try the following techniques if Rover doesn't want to SIT.

❏ Make sure your signaling hand is close to but not touching his face. It should be a few inches over his head.

❏ You could be standing too far away from him. Try stepping in.

❏ He may need traction. Instead of working on a slippery surface, use carpet or grass.

❏ Rover might be a leaner. Allow him to back into something solid, such as a piece of furniture, a wall, or a tree.

❏ He may feel vulnerable. A strong SIT is a sign of self-assurance. Although this is more of a behavioral issue than a training issue, working with him here may bolster his confidence elsewhere.

❏ If poor old Rover has hip dysplasia or is arthritic, sitting may be painful for him. In this case, clearly you should skip this command.

## Stay

I'm a stickler for STAY. Whether your dog is standing, sitting, or lying down, STAY means "Don't move from that spot until I release you." There are two ways to release Rover: You can either return to him or call him to come to you. Because STAY and COME are both potentially life-saving exercises but are essentially opposite concepts—no matter what *don't move* versus no matter what *move*—I prefer not to teach them too close together lest the puppy get the two confused. Only after STAY is mastered do I actively work on COME. I do, however, informally work on COME from day one by kneeling down and calling him when he's coming toward me anyway. When I lived in Tanzania, I learned Swahili at the same time as the tribal dialect of Chagga and I inevitably got my words mixed up. This could have been avoided if I had perfected one before learning the other. So it is with STAY and COME.

I prefer to teach this command off leash since it's more natural, but for safety's sake you might need to put a squirmy pup on a lightweight lead so that you can step on it should he try to take off. The leash here is a safety net that will enable you to proceed faster than you would without it; however, since it is our goal to have Rover stay without the leash, begin to phase it out as soon as it is safe to do so.

I'll talk you through SIT STAY as it's usually the easiest of the STAY commands to teach, but the process for teaching STAY is the same whatever your puppy's position. Once the puppy can SIT reliably, briefly praise him for doing so (this is old news by now), and then say STAY, just once, while signaling with your hand. Your voice should be clipped, almost staccato. The hand signal is the universal one for STOP used by traffic cops and Diana Ross's Supremes; your palm faces out, fingers pointing up. Say and sign STAY concurrently while you stand still. Count to three, then pet his chest and tell him what a good boy he is. Now offer a toy or treat. Use mediocre toys and bland treats at first, as the really cool stuff may be too exciting.

The message now is that if you STAY, good things will happen. In fact, STAY will soon become implicit in SIT, as a quick SIT is of limited usefulness. Occasionally, grasp Rover's collar from below while praising him to teach him that, in an emergency, this is a possible outcome. If, for example, your dog ran across a busy street, he would have to STAY there while you crossed over and grabbed hold of him.

47

Saying STAY just once encourages his attentiveness. Less is more here. He'll tune out if you drone on in a Muzak-like way, "STAY, STAY, STAY." Also note that it's best to simply say STAY without using his name. Why? Many dogs associate their names with action. STAY, of course, is the absence of activity. "Rover STAY" sounds like "Move, *don't* move" to many dogs.

By standing still right next to or in front of Rover when telling him to STAY, you show him where to be. If you want him to STAY at the front door but don't say STAY until you're ten feet outside it, how's a dog to understand? Delayed timing here could be disastrous, as this affords him ample opportunity to take off.

Once Rover understands the concept of STAY, slowly increase both the duration and distance. Ask him to STAY for ten seconds, thirty, and then a minute, from two feet, five feet, and then ten. The objective is to make the training easy enough that he can succeed, but tough enough that he will improve, and always quit on a high note.

Here, then, is how you teach Rover to stay: With the dog sitting, say and signal STAY (then count 2, 3), take a step back (2, 3), and return. "Good boys" abound. The "(2, 3)" is to help with the timing. It is important to pet under his head as reaching over it may be interpreted as a dominance challenge and cause him to shrink away from you. Now, back up as far as you can but stop short of tugging on the lead while he STAYS (2, 3), then return to him and reward. Next, drop the lead so you can step on it if necessary while Rover STAYS, and gradually build up his staying endurance. If your pup breaks, say "No!" then immediately redirect him back to the original spot by patting or pointing to it. The trick is to catch him in motion so that he makes the connection between the "No" and his action. Then start all over, nicely: Rover SIT, "Good boy," STAY (2, 3), back away (2, 3), and return. The quick switching from the harsh "No!" to a soft SIT is essential.

When this is going well, begin to push him by adding distractions. The point here is to test your dog, not drive him crazy. Distractions for a beginner could include kicking a leaf or adjusting a chair. Advance, when appropriate, to lifting his food bowl, squeaking a toy, or opening the door. Don't talk to Rover while he's staying, as you both need to concentrate.

How fast you can progress varies vastly. In a group class recently it took only ten minutes to teach Kelso, a Border collie cross, to STAY

### STAY TROUBLE-SHOOTING TIPS

#### 1. What if Rover lies down during a SIT STAY?

Rover is settling in for the long haul. This is a no-no in formal obedience training, but I consider it a bonus, because the DOWN STAY is almost always harder to teach. It's like being given $10 when you only asked for $5; if Rover offers the DOWN STAY for free, I wouldn't complain. You could be really clever and say DOWN as he's lying down to get a jump-start on our next lesson.

#### 2. What if Rover gets up as you are returning to him?

If he moves *toward* you, make sure you're not praising him too soon or otherwise talking to him, he may interpret your voice as a release. Also, try to contain your pride until you make contact and release him, as Rover may be overeager to receive your accolades. If he *backs away*, it could be that you're intimidating him by reaching your hand over, not under, his head. Also, if Rover associates your moving toward him with his being grabbed or punished, he will want to avoid making contact. This situation may be tough to turn around. In this case I'd recommend making your return to him ultra-fabulous, loving him up with your hands and offering good treats.

amid all the other dogs and people while I bounced a ball and ate a (people) cookie, yet I've been working privately for weeks with an English bulldog, Bella, who still won't STAY.

The continuous use of the STAY hand signal can be phased out in time, but use it consistently when teaching Rover to STAY, and flash it periodically thereafter as a reminder.

I like to make a distinction between STAY and WAIT. I know I said that the words you choose don't matter, and they don't. The point is to use two different words, whatever they are. STAY is of limited duration; you mark its completion. WAIT is open-ended; it means you can't come with me, but you *can* move. So, when I leave in the morning, I tell my dogs they have to WAIT. This keeps them from darting out the door. Saying STAY in this instance would only set them up to fail (I have also heard stories of very obedient dogs who were in the exact same position when their people returned hours later). Additionally, if STAY is synonymous with "Ma won't be home for a long time," an anxious dog may panic upon hearing it and not STAY when it's essential he do so. I believe this is Bella the bulldog's problem.

> **Beware the STAY itch: This mysterious little tickle has been known to show up on dogs around the world when they've had it with STAY. This itch on their neck, near an ear, miraculously disappears when STAY is ended. Displaced nervous energy manifests in many species as self-grooming. We humans chew our nails and twirl our hair; birds pluck their feathers; cats lick; and dogs get this STAY itch. An open-minded pup may even lick and chew too.**

### Down

Teaching a dog to lie DOWN can be difficult. It seems paradoxical that asking Rover to assume the most comfortable of positions would cause so much resistance in so many dogs, but it does. Different dogs dislike following this command for different reasons: High-energy pups don't like being told to be still; dominant dogs don't want to assume this passive posture; and submissive ones feel too vulnerable. That covers just about most dogs.

Many significant problems can be solved by teaching your dog DOWN. Typically, the degree to which a dog resists this exercise is proportionate to the importance of his learning it. Between dogs, lying DOWN can show contrition, submission, respect, and an inferior rank. Many roll over to expose their genitals as though to say, "There's nothing hidden here." Some even release a little urine. That's as low as you can go.

An easy, albeit slow, way to teach this tricky exercise is to back into it. Say DOWN when you observe Rover spontaneously lying down. He initiates the action; you just have to be watchful. Consider it a freebie; he was lying DOWN anyway. This is one way that both dogs and humans learn language; for example, if you say "clap" every time the baby puts her hands together, in short order the word "clap" will prompt her to do so. You may get lucky and catch Rover lying down ten or twenty times a day. Say DOWN while he's in motion, not once he's there. You're naming the *action,* not the position. Saying DOWN after Rover's been prone for a while is to label whatever else he's doing when he hears the word: "Does DOWN mean lick my foot? Belch?" Remember that timing is critical.

This passive approach, which can be used with other exercises as well, isn't always practical. A more proactive method of teaching Rover to LIE DOWN is to lure him there. So far, we've used treats—food and toys—as a reward; now we will use them as bait. Although an empty hand scooping up and over your dog's head is usually enough to lure him to SIT, you may need a treat to get him DOWN. But in the spirit of our Economics of Dog Training, try to get him to do it for free first by doing the following:

With Rover sitting on his bed or favorite sleeping spot, lower your hand from his nose to the surface directly below, as though there's a string attached that you're pulling straight down. This gesture will become the DOWN hand signal. Wiggle your fingers and pat or rub the floor below him. No talking: He needs to focus on your hand, not your mouth. Most dogs express their curiosity by mouthing, pawing, or staring at your fingers. These are good signs that he's engaged. When he has begun actively sniffing your hand, slowly slide it along the floor away from Rover, which will maneuver him into the DOWN position. No force, no resistance. So long as Rover is interested in your hand, this will eventually work, I promise. Be patient; it may take a few minutes.

The use of material lures—toys and food—comes into play if Rover is totally ignoring your naked hand. In this case, instead of wiggling your fingers simply hold the treat and get him to follow the goodie DOWN and then out. Now tell him what a brilliant boy he is and give him the treat. You should be next to Rover, not looming over him, as this may make him uneasy. Also make sure that you don't step backwards between saying SIT and DOWN, as he will step forward to follow you.

Once the DOWN is solid, keep Rover there with the STAY. The trick to transitioning into the STAY is to calmly praise the DOWN and immediately, in the same breath, say STAY, "Good boy, STAY." Don't leave enough time for him to pop up. From this point, the particulars of cultivating the DOWN STAY are the same as those for SIT STAY.

Your goal is to push him to twenty minutes. It may take a week or two, but stick with it. Mastery here is guaranteed to transform your relationship with your dog. He can now be free on his own recognizance while you have dinner or watch the news. Think of this as an invisible crate. The long DOWN STAY will enable you to take him where he was previously unwelcome: into stores, your in-laws', soccer games, and barbecues. Just imagine how much more pleasant your next visit to the vet will be. While staying down, Rover is free to play with a toy, read a book, whatever. You wouldn't tell your kid *not* to do her homework while relegated to her room.

In no circumstance is the long DOWN STAY more appreciated than when you are teaching your dog not to beg. I don't know about you, but I can't stand a begging dog. My kuvasz, Kiana, was two years old and out of control when I adopted her. My home was her fourth. Kiana didn't just beg; the ninety-pound dog stood on the kitchen table. I fixed this by first teaching her to lie DOWN and STAY on a little throw rug in the kitchen. Next, I advanced to putting food on the table while she stayed and slowly built up her tolerance here. When Kiana tried to stand up—which she often did—I'd say "No!" and immediately redirect her nicely back to the mat. Then I feigned eating with her lying DOWN. This was simulated simply because I needed to be free to act fast if she broke. Once we succeeded at this, I was mercifully able to actually eat while she stayed down.

It's best to practice this over a bowl of cereal at first, not at a birthday dinner, as you need to correct every transgression. Even with a wild woman like Kiana, it only took a week. Conditioning

### THE PRONATED WRIST

Look for Rover to fold, or pronate, his wrist once he is lying down and settled. This is a curious piece of involuntary body language that tells you he's at ease. Indeed, for the dangerous dog and one who is especially resistant to lying DOWN, pronation is the canine equivalent of saying "Uncle."

Kiana to lie DOWN on that inexpensive, lightweight, washable rug created a portable target. Whether in the kitchen, the dining room, at a neighbor's house, in dog class, or at a sidewalk café, its presence suggested DOWN.

When Rover has mastered DOWN STAY, it's time to teach him to GO LIE DOWN, a.k.a. GOLD. You'll love this. A chain of multiple behaviors such as GOLD is best taught backwards. Here this means first teaching him where to lie DOWN. This can vary from room to room, and from season to season. A whippet will welcome a cozy bed to curl up on in the winter while a Samoyed seeks out the air-conditioning vent when it's hot.

Catch Rover en route to his favorite place and say GO LIE DOWN. If he does this often enough while you are watching, no more direction may be needed. Otherwise, escort your dog to his designated place from progressively greater distances, starting at about three feet. Hands off. Simply encourage him to follow by making kissing or clicking sounds and patting your leg with one hand as you walk to and pat the bed. The GO hand signal is an exaggerated, underhand pointing gesture.

GO LIE DOWN is a nice way to say "leave me alone." I came home recently with a horrible headache and wasn't up to giving my dogs as much attention as they're used to getting. So I gave each a chew bone and asked them to GO LIE DOWN. It was as if I had popped *101 Dalmatians* in the VCR to entertain the kids; I was a hero and nobody's feelings were hurt.

## Come

Getting Rover to COME when called is the ultimate test of your ability to think like a dog. If coming to you is better than his other options, then COME to you he will, so long as you've taken the time to teach him what the word means.

Those of you with puppies under five months old may be wondering, "What's the big deal? Rover's always hanging around." I caution you against getting lulled into a false sense of security; things are about to change.

Dogs are domesticated wolves. Your toy poodle is as much a wolf as is a malamute. A wolf could mate with a Chihuahua—though I'm

53

not sure why he'd want to—and have viable offspring. "Hybrids" they're called. And although the dog has come a long way since being domesticated, scratch the surface and you've got a wolf.

In the wild, a mother wolf would never sell her puppies at eight weeks just because they were weaned and she could use the cash. She'd keep the family together for at least a year to teach the kids how to hunt, make a den, and earn a living. Then, when the pups approached sexual maturity, it would be time for the strong ones to disperse lest they inbreed.

Although a wolf only comes into heat once a year and not before she's a year old, dog breeders have manipulated genes so as to maximize puppy production, with a puppy's first biannual cycle potentially occurring as early as six months. The puppies, with hormones raging, are now subject to the same primal, biological imperative of their wolf relatives. Like all teenagers, they want to take off. This is what I call the "flight phase."

Recently, I arrived at a first-time client's house on an extremely busy road during rush hour traffic. The five-month-old Irish setter, O'Grady, ran up to my car to say hello. I immediately expressed concern to O'Grady's person about the puppy's proximity to the road, flight phase and all. It was apparent from the man's demeanor that he was annoyed by my interference. He'd never had a problem, after all. That very night, O'Grady was killed by a truck right in front of his house. More on the flight phase later; I just wanted to make sure those with prepubescent pups read on.

People seem to assume that puppies should innately know what's expected of them when you open the back door and yell COME. They don't. So first I am going to talk you through the technique, which is the easy part, and then I will explain the all-important but elusive psychology of getting your dog to COME when called.

### THE TECHNIQUE

Food is necessary in teaching Rover to COME. There's a lot of competition out there: cats to be chased, goose poop to be rolled in, dogs to hump. Adorable though you might be, your charm is not enough; you need food. Some people consider this selling out. So they try and try to get Rover to COME, then eventually break down and "resort to bribing him with food." What this effectively does is teach the dog to hold out. Why would Rover COME for free when he could wait a while and hit pay dirt? I tell my clients that though they seem perfectly pleasant, I was only willing to COME to their house because I was getting paid. Seeing as you'll probably need it anyway, you might as well use food up front.

I have had fabulous results using clickers to teach dogs to COME. Once primed, Rover may well be attracted to its distinctive sound and actually seek it out. Experiment around the house by occasionally clicking and see if he comes. If so, lavish praise upon him, click again, and give him a treat. Remember that the click precedes the treat and is another way to say "Good boy!" I therefore find it helps to click when I praise. Don't worry if Rover dislikes the clicker or you find it too cumbersome; then don't use it. All of the following instructions apply to you equally. Simply ignore the "(click)."

Catch Rover moving toward you, kneel down with your arms spread wide, smile, and, in an upbeat voice, say, "Good boy! (click) Rover COME." Encourage him by clapping and cheering the whole way. When he arrives, love him up (click) and give him a treat. Rover can now go back to whatever he was doing. "COME means I get a piece of cheese and I still get to sunbathe. Hot dog!" Please remember not to click too close to his ears. And never use the clicker when he's in the midst of something you dislike.

After a few days of this, rather than waiting for Rover to initiate coming, it's time you call him. Again, kneel down and say, "Rover COME" (click), and "Good boy." Pet, praise, and feed him. Instead of food, sometimes give him a chew toy or throw a ball. With so many rewards, you can occasionally omit one or two while still reinforcing his behavior.

Coming is a process, not just the punch line. Sound upbeat as you encourage him all along the way. You don't want Rover to change his mind en route and take off. If you are physically able, kneeling down is important as it's ingratiating. Ever notice how, if you sit on the floor to snap Rover's photo, he comes over and licks the lens? With STAY I want you to stand tall; with COME, its opposite, smaller is better. Envision Rover coming to you. I know it's a little silly, but I swear it helps.

Capitalize on naturally occurring reinforcement. Have Rover COME for dinner, COME for a walk, COME out of his crate. Call him to COME into the car to drive to the beach and COME out of it once you're there. How cool is COME? Conversely, I say and signal GO to end the event: GO home, GO to the car, GO in your crate. Remember, rewards are to be randomized and occasionally withheld.

Some dogs do what I call the "drive-by." They'll COME, snatch the treat, and whoosh right past you. This can make you crazy. No dog. No treat. No good. In this case, still love him up verbally for coming but withhold the treat. Stand up. Ask Rover to SIT, say "Good boy" (click), *now* give him a cookie. Wait a few seconds, (click), hand him another treat, another few seconds, another treat. Keep this up for about a minute. Having him SIT before he gets a cookie buys you time to grab hold of his collar from below in an emergency. All those treats are to demonstrate that it's worth his hanging around awhile.

Practice COME indoors and out with minimal distractions at first, ideally in a fenced yard. If that's not possible, for safety's sake,

## LETTING YOUR DOG OFF LEASH

As a professional, I cannot condone dogs running free where there are leash laws. It is dangerous and not neighborly. Nor can I guarantee that the techniques taught here, or anywhere, will keep your dog safe. That said, as a dog lover, my greatest joy is watching my dogs run free. Of course, I take every precaution in training them and selecting safe areas to exercise them. And I never, ever take their wild spirit for granted.

There are dogs who are simply not reliable off leash. Certain breeds, notably sled dogs, were specifically bred by humans to run. In my experience, Siberian huskies are especially flighty. Beagles aren't great, either. Any dog, however, could prove to be reliable or unreliable off leash, no matter what the breed. Kiana, the kuvasz I adopted at two years from her third family, is one such dog. Judging from her panicked response, I assume she was previously mistreated upon coming. The trauma is too deeply imprinted for me to be able to reverse it. It breaks my heart to keep Kiana on a leash while my other dogs run free on our Sunday morning woods walks. But I must.

Rover needs to be dragging around a lightweight twenty-foot rope so you can step on it should he try to take off. He must *never* be on a choke chain and you must *always* be there to supervise. Small dogs and those with delicate tracheas should be wearing a harness.

Once Rover appears to grasp the concept, the hand signal will become a pulling toward you gesture, as though reeling him in, which you may need to do gently if ornery Rover refuses to budge. Don't drag him; just coax him along. No matter how he gets to you, be ever so happy that he did. After two weeks, gradually wean him off the rope by incrementally shortening it, until you can eliminate it altogether.

Get the whole family involved. The beauty of using clickers is that everyone has the same click. (If your kids are too young to realize that clickers are not toys, however, it's best they don't use them.) Play hide-and-seek (you hide, Rover seeks). Make it fun, but *don't* run after him. Whoever is being chased is in charge. The top dog always leads a sled dog team. It is fine if Rover runs after you, but your chasing him not only conveys the wrong message, it also teaches him to run away from you. This can be deadly. I have known of two dogs who were chased in front of cars by their families. *Please remember this in an emergency.* If Rover refuses to COME, get his attention any way you can—clap your hands, shake a biscuit box, jiggle the car keys, whatever—and run *away* from him. Hopefully this will tap into his desire to chase and he'll come a runnin'. I cannot guarantee this will work, but I promise that chasing defiant Rover won't, unless of course you can corner him.

### THE PSYCHOLOGY

It is often in early puppyhood that we inadvertently teach dogs *not* to COME when called. Let's say baby Rover has been left free in the kitchen while you shower. At 8:15 he knocks over the trash while you're shampooing your hair. At 8:40, you enter the kitchen, discover the garbage, and call Rover over to it. When he gets to you, you yell at him or, worse, spank him. Since twenty-five minutes have elapsed, the puppy has no idea you're mad at his making a mess. He thinks it's the last thing he did, the coming, that got him into trouble.

This example is pretty obvious. What's less so is that we often use COME only to mean that a good thing has come to an end. Let's say you take Rover to the park for his daily exercise. He's having a ball romping with the other dogs, digging trenches, and chasing chipmunks. The one and only time he hears "Rover COME," it means, "Stop playing with the other puppies. It's time to go home." The same problem could arise if Rover's out in his fenced yard for an hour and a half in the morning while the family gets ready for the day. Believing you're being generous, you wait until the very last moment to call Rover in. Then, in a hurried frenzy, you order him to COME, only to lock him up and leave for the day. In these instances COME means getting spanked, leaving the park, isolation, and abandonment. Not coming means pain-free fun and freedom. Which would you choose?

Obviously, life goes on and Rover has to learn to fit in. It's just that these are not the times to teach him to COME. The optimal time to teach is when you know you'll succeed.

So how should you have handled the three scenarios described above? When the puppy tipped over the garbage while you shampooed, you should have ignored it. These things happen. Perhaps he should be crated tomorrow. Better yet, have him hang out in the bathroom with you.

At the dog park, rather than waiting until it was time to leave to use the command COME, you should have spent the first few minutes reviewing COME. Consider it a rehearsal. And make sure he knows you've got good eats. Then call Rover periodically throughout your time at the park, lavishly love him up for coming, offer a treat intermittently, and let him go back and play with the other dogs. If you call Rover ten times during the thirty-minute outing, and only one time means "we're leaving," you will diminish his perceived negative consequence to coming when called. These are odds any betting mutt would take. And don't wait until the very last second to call him. Do so a few minutes prior to leaving, give him a reward, put the leash on, and GO home or to the car. And remember, so long as you are supervising, there is nothing wrong with leaving a lightweight rope on Rover until you iron out the kinks.

When you're calling Rover in so you can leave in the morning, or whenever, call him twenty minutes before it's time for you to go. Of course, richly reward his coming. Then give him something to chew and calmly leave as usual. Those twenty minutes are enough for him to disconnect coming with being left. Not to worry, this twenty-minute cushion can eventually be reduced when mature Rover has learned the drill.

**POP QUIZ**

**Question:** It is 11 P.M. You let Rover out for the last time before going to bed. Unbeknownst to you, the kids forgot to close the gate and Rover escapes. By the time you realize this, he's long gone. In the distance you hear screeching brakes. Rover? If only you'd taken the vet's advice and had him neutered. Three-and-a-half panic-filled hours later Rover returns with a deep gash on his side, having rolled in something rank, smoking a cigarette, and reeking of gin. What do you do?

**Answer:** Reward him.

That's right; reward him. Of course, you may want to throttle the SOB. But we are thinking like a dog here. The last thing Rover did was come home, and unless this behavior is richly rewarded, if he gets out again, he may not. His misbehavior—taking off—happened three-and-a-half blissful hours earlier. While away, our boy knocked up the Tibetan terrier around the corner, raided two garbage cans, and swam in a swamp. Puppy paradiso. Having sampled what's out there, Rover will be more motivated to escape in the future. I realize that simply rewarding his return and leaving it at that is eminently unsatisfying, so I'd also recommend intensively reviewing his training, especially STAY at the gate and COME when called. It's not clear what, if any, impact this will actually have, but at least you'll feel like you are doing something. Show Rover there's no place like home. Enrich the yard by tossing tiny treats around and hiding special toys. Play with and train him there. His grass Is the greenest. Many dogs will welcome a hard plastic kiddy pool in the summer. Try throwing a rope over a branch from which a choice toy is suspended. If he's relegated to hang out by himself too long with nothing to do, escaping may be a way to lessen the loneliness and boredom. I'd also suggest installing a spring hinge on the gate. And get romantic Rover neutered.

Be sure you are not angrily yelling COME! when you're upset about what he's doing or scared about what he might do. Unlike "No," which signals what you don't want him to do and must sound stern, COME should be said in a nice voice. The bottom line is that when your dog is off lead he has the upper hand, and he knows it. The eternal opportunist, Rover is assessing the cost and benefits of coming to you at every juncture. Your job is to make it worth his while, or he won't.

## HEEL

HEEL is simply the word used for "Walk." Dogs are meant to walk at their master's *heel,* their shoulder even with your knee. Give me a break. In this book HEEL means controlled walking. If you'd prefer, say "Walk" or "Let's go." HEEL is the most unnatural of exercises. Wild canids SIT, LIE DOWN, STAY, and even COME when their wolf mothers call, but walk on lead on the left side sans pulling? I don't think so.

When I started training dogs in New York City, teaching them to HEEL was a priority. Walking on a leash is a fact of an urban dog's life. In Connecticut, this is largely a lost art. With the advent of underground fences, people can contain their dogs at home in a cost-effective way. These and conventional fences have made many of us lazy. I typically tell my clients that even if they don't have to walk their dogs, being able to walk on a leash is an important skill well-rounded Rover should learn. Too often, people never walk their dogs because they *can't,* not because they choose not to. This is a shame.

Because HEEL is so unnatural an exercise to teach, a bit of pre-training will go a long way. When baby Rover is about three months,

HEEL is like a dance; both you and your dog need to be attentive to one another's body language and anticipate the other's next move. As choreographer, your goal is to motivate Rover to want to walk nicely because it is pleasurable to do—it is a fabulous feeling to be so in sync as to walk together gracefully—and to convey that there are consequences to his not.

put a lightweight leash on him for a few minutes here and there and simply allow him to become familiar with this strange string. Once the novelty has worn off, walk away from him purposefully. Puppies are natural followers, so he will probably follow after you, dragging the leash behind. Good boy! After a few days of this, pick up the lead and encourage him to walk with you. If he balks, simply drop the leash for now and try again in a day or two. Should baby Rover prance along, stop every twenty seconds or so and praise him lovingly. Walk him on over to his food bowl and his best toys. Keep this game up for about five days.

It is totally natural for a dog to pull. That you are yanked is incidental to his checking out the weimaraner walking his way. So job number one is to teach Rover that he's pulling you and that you don't like it. HEEL is the one exercise where equipment beyond toys and treats is often necessary. I no longer use choke collars. When used irresponsibly, they could crush a dog's trachea or cause him to choke to death. In the old days, I didn't know better and there were few alternatives. Now, I prefer the following, safer choices. I will discuss the pluses and minuses of each, and you can make your own choice.

### ACCESSORIES
#### Harnesses

It is safer to walk a small dog, and some big ones, using a harness rather than a collar. Because small dogs are so low to the ground, a collar will inevitably be pulled up, thereby threatening their delicate throats. Hacking, choking coughs can be a sign of tracheal damage, which may be irreversible. A regular harness will spare Rover's throat but might actually encourage him to pull. There are a number of antipull harnesses on the market that prevent pulling without causing any pain. Sporn is the brand with which I am most familiar. I've seen great results with many small and some medium to large dogs using this halter.

There are, however, a few downsides to using no-pull harnesses:

**61**

- They can be annoying to put on and take off a fidgety puppy.

- I have heard of dogs chewing through their straps.

### Headcollars

The Gentle Leader and Halti are two brands of nylon head halters that go over a dog's muzzle and actually control his head, much like halters used on horses. These clever, pain-free devices discourage pulling and can have a calming effect on dogs once they're accustomed to wearing one. Herein the rub. The acclimation period can be lengthy, with some dogs wiping their faces along the ground or pawing at the halter in an attempt to get this alien contraption off. This can be so disconcerting to watch that I've known many people who gave up on them prematurely. The other problem with head halters is one of PR. They look like muzzles and often turn onlookers off, convincing them your dog is dangerous. A major advantage to using a halter is that, because they control the dog's head, they enable you to pull a lunging, snapping dog's mouth away from anyone he might bite.

### Pinch Collars

These collars, with their double rows of teeth, look like medieval torture devices. For at least fifteen years, I sanctimoniously decried the evils of these cruel-looking collars, while actively promoting choke collars. Now, with great humility and tail between legs, I must confess that for the large, drag-you-across-the-street-without-looking-back career puller for whom the other options have proven ineffective or too stressful, I have come to love pinch collars. Love them! I hate that I love them so much. Phew. Out of the closet at last. I've actually been terrified to write this chapter because I knew I'd have to tell you this.

The beauty of these collars is that they are self-limiting. Unlike a choke collar, they can only tighten so far. And because the degree of tightening is directly related to the intensity of the pulling, the severity of the pinch is 100 percent controlled by Rover. There can be absolutely no confusion as to why he was corrected (and if he never pulls he is never corrected). Because the prong collar is jagged, it can't compress Rover's trachea as the solid strap of even an everyday buckle-type cloth collar can. I regularly hear testimonials from people who had resisted trying one and can now walk their previously unmanageable dogs. The gentlest of corrections gets results.

The following, however, are the problems with pinch collars:

- Their look. Talk about turning people off! I sure wish they came in pink.

- In the wrong hands, there is potential for abuse.

### Weighing Your Options

The decision to use a no-pull harness, a head halter, or a pinch collar is a personal one. Here, as everywhere, pursue the gentlest approach that works. Still, I believe it is kinder to walk a dog using special equipment than to leave him home if he can't do without it. The pinch collar is the harshest of the three options, so I only recommend using it as a last resort and only with puppies over six months. Though the head halter is not painful, the frustration some dogs experience wearing it can also be viewed as aversive. And, as benign as the no-pull harness is, I have known many people who find them too awkward to put on.

### *GETTING DOWN TO BUSINESS*

First we'll teach Rover the technique, and then we'll take it on the road. Much in the way that your child learns to ride a bicycle in the driveway, your dog should learn to HEEL in a controlled environment before going out on a test drive. Traditionally, dogs are taught to HEEL on the person's left side. This mattered when choke collars were used. For our purposes, just select one side or the other so as to prevent Rover's wrapping you up. Use a four- or six-foot cloth or leather leash. Four is easier to use because you simply have to hold the handle. A six-foot leash is more versatile but needs to be shortened by doubling up. Retractable leashes are too cumbersome for teaching HEEL. Don't use any special collars or harnesses for now. A regular harness, however, is appropriate at any point.

Assuming Rover is on your left side, step away, leading with your left leg while you pat it and make clicking or kissing sounds. Hold the (shortened) leash in your right hand over your belly button. There should be enough slack for it to drape comfortably in front of you. Take a few steps forward, cooing all the way, and stop. Ask Rover to SIT, say "Good boy," and give him a cookie for sitting. Walk on. This time, go forward, then turn around and walk the other way. If our boy's attentive enough to turn with you, praise him to the nines! This is what we're after. Coax Rover along as you speed up and slow down. Turn to the right and the left. It's a dizzying experience that's meant to make his tending to you safer and more interesting than whatever else is going on. Remember playing Red Light/Green Light? Not knowing when the light would change colors was what made it fun. Instead of kissing sounds you could chat or sing. Tell Rover a joke. I know you feel like a fool. No one said dog training was dignified.

In the beginning, a few minutes at a stretch is enough, though you can work at it many times a day. Once Rover seems hooked into this new game, say HEEL when stepping away. We're teaching him a foreign language. As you would enunciate especially clearly when speaking to someone who only knew Italian, exaggerate your body language here to help him to catch on. Step away confidently, pat your leg with gusto, stop, and turn dramatically. Bravo!

The best way to teach Rover not to lunge forward is to anticipate his doing so and turn around. Should he turn with you, accolades abound. If he trudges onward—*darn*—he gets a correction. This could have been completely avoided, had he only been paying attention. The severity of the correction is commensurate with the speed with which Rover pulls away from you. Rushing ahead at five miles per hour is five times more jarring than it is at one mile per hour. If you are unsteady on your feet or if it's slippery, simply stop rather than turning around. Pull the leash in toward your belly and bend your knees, thereby anchoring yourself and protecting your torso. When Rover hits the end of the leash say "No!" Then immediately, no matter how mad you are, go back to your nice voice and ask him to HEEL. Always correct then redirect. Gradually increase the number of steps you take forward before stopping or turning around.

A serviceable formula to follow at any impasse is to move in the opposite direction. This encourages Rover to check in. When he forges forward, you go backwards; he jumps up, you snap down. Should he pull left, turn to the right. If Rover refuses to walk or lags behind, jog ahead. Don't drag him; this will only create more resistance. Move along enticingly so that he'll want to catch up.

## TAKING IT ON THE ROAD

Allow the first few minutes out of the house to be (fairly) free-form. This will take the edge off his energy and will make tightening the reins easier to do. Next, spend a few minutes reviewing HEEL before actually beginning the walk. Rover needs to SIT and STAY at the end of your driveway and at curbs prior to crossing the street. This habit could save his life. Try tapping your left foot or doing a little dip before saying SIT. This flourish will come to signal the changing of gears and may hasten Rover's learning to automatically SIT when you stop.

Having Rover HEEL is an efficient way to get from here to there, but heeling is not all there is to taking him out. How's a dog to poop or get the neighborhood scoop if he's prancing along like a prince? Dogs live to sniff. It's as enriching for them as looking is for us. Allow him to stop and smell *some* things; we just have to teach him that he can't smell *everything*. You decide whether to cover ten blocks with two stops or two blocks with ten stops. Not all outings are for exercise; some can be about gathering information.

When it's time to move along smartly, ask Rover to HEEL. Turning around is the best way to bring his attention back to you. Occasionally, preempt pulling by having him SIT. This changes the subject, reminds him that you are in charge, and gives you an opportunity to offer a reward. Release Rover to sniff and relieve himself by saying, "Okay, be a dog." When it's time to move on, ask him to HEEL again. And so it goes. In time, these formal steps will become comfortable patterns that make walking Rover a joy.

Holding your dog in place with a tight leash simply teaches him to tolerate tension. The goal is to motivate him to hold himself in place, which can only be accomplished with a loose leash. Rover, not you, should be doing the work. Allow the leash to be slack throughout the walk except for during that split second when his pulling makes it taut. That's when you bark "No!" wait a few seconds, and then nicely say, "Rover, HEEL." The causal relationship between his pulling and being corrected is unmistakable.

While maintaining a loose, relaxed leash, hold it securely so that you're prepared for challenges encountered along the way. If you see another dog headed toward you, in an upbeat, jolly voice say, "Here comes a beautiful basset hound," and trot along with a loose leash at the same pace as before. There's an old dog training adage that the han-

**65**

dler's anxiety is transmitted through the leash, and it's true. If you tense up upon seeing the hound and nervously bark HEEL, HEEL, HEEL, or yank Rover over to the side of the road, the message is that the other dog's approach is a worrisome thing. Because you seem to be a wreck, Rover may either choose to fight with this dog who has upset you so, or run and hide from him. It is the most natural thing in the world for dogs to want to say hello to each other. Why wouldn't they? Preventing this creates frustration that often manifests in aggression. Clearly, we have no control over the other dog's, or person's, social skills, which is why it's wise to hope for the best while being braced for the worst.

### TWO DOG-WALKING TIPS

• If you walk in a residential area without sidewalks, as I often do, when the occasional car drives by, say something like "Out of the road," and hurry your dog onto the grass where he is asked to SIT. "Good boy!" Conditioning Rover to get out of the way of moving vehicles by seeking the grass may ultimately prove life saving.

• At the end of the walk, enthusiastically say and signal "Go home!" as you approach the house. Instead of just making a big deal about going for a walk, you should also create some excitement about its ending. (Similarly, if you drive Rover to a park, say "Go to the car" when you're ready to leave.) Once the dog is inside the house or car, give him a treat to associate with his actions. This might even help someday motivate a Roving Rover to return home.

## CHAPTER 5

# The Games Dogs Play: For Whom the Ball Rolls

For Rover, as for a human, play is the basis for learning.

You just haven't lived until you watch a puppy dodge waves on the beach, catch a Frisbee midflight, or roll in fresh snow with gleeful abandon. Play is more than adorable; it is central to the healthy development of adult behavior. It is a rehearsal of sorts, during which the consequences of one's actions are first learned. Bite your brother's tail too hard and he won't be your best friend. If you don't stand up for yourself, you'll be the last to eat. A study of convicted murderers on death row in Texas showed that 90 percent either didn't play at all as children or played sadistically.

Play can be solitary or interactive, involving objects or not. Structured play enhances specific skills; free-form play encourages independence and originality. Both types are necessary for balance. I think it's tragic that many children have such hectic schedules that they're denied time to just be kids. I have a number of type A clients who rear their dogs the same way.

Richard left a voice mail message for me the other day asking to set up an appointment to "teach his dog to play." This was not the usual request; most people complain about their dogs being *too* playful. Having met previously abused dogs who didn't play, I assumed this dog would have the same problem. When we finally spoke, Richard explained that his two-year-old Swiss mountain dog, Yodel, only wanted to hang out with the kids, ride in the car, chew his bones, and bird-watch in the backyard. "And the problem with that would be?" Richard had high hopes that Yodel would run with him, yet the dog's interests were more sedentary. Jogging was Richard's kind of fun, not Yodel's. Dogs play for their own entertainment, not ours.

A woman began our first session by saying, "I love dogs; I just don't like when they do doggy things." I swear to God. Her house was

**69**

organized with military precision; the belongings and scheduled events of each of her four children were color-coded, and everything was exactly where it belonged. On top of the long list of "doggy things" she didn't like was the way her four-month-old cairn terrier, Chompsky, chewed his toys. The shredding was unsightly.

I paid an emergency Sunday morning house call to visit a young couple that had recently moved in together. His vizsla and her flat-coated retriever were "fighting to the death." And despite the fact that neither had so much as nicked the other in the two weeks they had cohabited, the couple "couldn't cope." Both brutes were sequestered in their respective corners when I arrived. After twenty tearful minutes spent strategizing, with great trepidation and crisis intervention plans in place, we let the warring factions have at it. After greeting me, the dogs began to wrestle. "See! They're going to kill each other!" she screamed while he wrenched the two apart. Not only were these dogs not fighting, they weren't even playing especially roughly. This is what two dogs do. You want they should play mah-jongg? The toughest part of the session was figuring out how to fill the remaining time.

Yodel's play interests, Chompsky's chewing style, and the room-mates' jostling are three examples of dogs happily being dogs. Control freaks have a hard time accepting this. That Yodel entertained himself was a perfect fit for Richard's overly scheduled family who were never home. Chomp's eviscerating his toys was preferable to him shredding anything else in that perfect house. And so long as the cohabitants were allowed to work things out through play fighting, chances were good matters would never escalate. How puppies play amongst themselves and with toys is dog controlled. It is in playing with us that tutelage may be warranted, specifically tug-of-war and retrieving.

## Tug-of-War

The long-standing common wisdom has been to ban tug-of-war (TOW) across the board as it's reputed to make dogs aggressive. And it is true to a point: The unschooled dog may become overstimulated and get too rough and TOW you across the room, while another could lose his grip on the toy and mistakenly grab hold of your hand. Playing tug-of-war with their dogs may therefore be inappropriate for children and the elderly.

On the other hand, I have observed infant puppies as young as eighteen days old tugging with their littermates. To deny a dog an activity that is so natural runs the risk of causing the repressed behavior to manifest elsewhere. Think of parents refusing their son toy guns only to discover him forming one with his fingers. So rather than throwing out the puppy with the bathwater, let's teach Rover how to play tug-of-war safely.

Before starting to play tug-of-war, your pup needs to learn to SIT and to DROP as if you were teaching him quid pro quo (page 77–81). Wave a designated tug toy flirtatiously in front of Rover. When he grabs hold say something like, "You wanna tug?" After a few seconds of tugging, ask him to SIT, say "Good boy," DROP, and give him a cookie. Repeat this several times, then say something like, "That's all," and put the toy away. The point is for you to be in control of when you play, for how long, and with what. If Rover gets too rough, game's over. Just walk away. If you haven't established these parameters, young Rover may decide to tug the towel you're draped in or pull the mitten off your daughter's hand.

Tug-of-war can be very empowering for the meek dog. When I first adopted my shy dog Monty, the Dobuki (Doberman/saluki mix), I gently encouraged his grabbing hold of the tug toy and then I released it with great fanfare and told him what a big, brave boy he was

## Retrieving

We all have this L. L. Bean image of our dogs blissfully retrieving all the ding-dong day. And, of course, lots of dogs love to fetch. And a lot don't. The chasing piece is a no-brainer. Puppies are programmed to run after fast-moving objects. It's the picking up, bringing back, and dropping that's a challenge. Rather than trying to force round Rover into the retrieving square, first assess his aptitude and your own commitment, and then teach him the rules.

When a dog learns a multistep exercise, he must first understand each element on its own. Coordinating the components comes later. Like learning to swim, only after blowing bubbles, kicking, and arm movements are mastered can they be integrated into the breaststroke. I like teaching behavior chains backwards. In this case, this means rehearsing DROP first. Before asking him to DROP, say SIT, which reminds him that you-know-who is in charge. Bringing the ball back to you is COME. Picking it up is TAKE IT. We're assuming that running after the ball is of enough interest to Rover that no further instruction is necessary. If it isn't, play another game.

Here's how it works: Throw the toy and say FETCH or GO GET IT. When Rover gets to it, say TAKE IT, "Good boy!" Now it's COME or BRING IT HERE. "What a guy!" SIT. "Good dog!" DROP. Repeat. Repeat. Repeat. Repeat. Repeat. Repeat. Repeat. Repeat.

Retrieving is a handy interactive way to exercise Rover, especially where space is limited. Should he stop just short of returning to you as though to say, "Come and get me," don't. To do so rewards his playing hard to get. Simply walk away; the game's over. Some puppies prefer to run off with the captured prize only to settle down away from you for a leisurely chew. Most people hate this. I think it's cute. Remember, after all, for whom the ball rolls.

## CHAPTER 6

# Problem Solving

The ideal is for Rover to be so exquis-
itely trained that problems never
start. In the real world, however, the
vast majority of the thousands of
clients I have worked with over the
past twenty-three years need help
solving at least some of the following
problems.

The Bark Stops Here

## Jumping

I never met a puppy that didn't jump. Indeed, jumping is the number one complaint I'm called about. Whether it's on people, furniture, or the kitchen counter, jumping is annoying and potentially quite dangerous.

So why do dogs jump on us? To get to our faces. Dogs are domesticated wolves, and wolf pups leap up to lick their mother's mouth by way of asking her to please regurgitate a little elk. And she does. Another day, another doe, and the gestalt is complete. We unwittingly reinforce the puppy's behavior by lifting him, feeding him, or taking him outside when he jumps on us. Seeing as his biological mother got him started, it doesn't take much encouragement on our part to create a monster.

### HOW TO BEGIN

One of the best things about puppies is their wiggly-waggly delight in seeing us. Though you just took out the trash, a hero's welcome awaits you upon your return. Many of us respond to this greeting in one of three wrong ways:

1. We feed into the frenzy because we find his welcome flattering.

2. We overcorrect happy Rover, causing the confused puppy to cower or submissively urinate.

3. We ignore him, which frustrates the puppy, thereby amplifying his neediness.

**75**

The challenge, therefore, is to find a solution that allows for his enthusiasm while dissuading the jumping. Here's how:

With a brand-new, impressionable puppy for whom confidence building and bonding are paramount, simply kneel or sit on the floor when saying hello. Puppies live for this. A focused "How do you do" for a minute or two is enough. Lowering your face obviates his need to jump. Upon standing, ask him to SIT and calmly praise his doing so. Sitting is incompatible with jumping and demonstrates an acceptable way to say "Hey." Some super-squirmy puppies just can't contain themselves. They should be praised simply for keeping their four on the floor rather than sitting. At this stage, never take his *not* jumping when greeting for granted.

If the puppy jumps when you stand, step toward him as he becomes airborne. This is exactly the opposite of what he expects and throws him off his game. Don't back up. To do so is an invitation for him to advance. In attack training, the agitator nervously retreats to elicit the dog's aggression. Stepping into the puppy is a gentle way to use this dynamic to your advantage by causing *him* to back off. And, of course, end the exchange with SIT. Attaboy!

For the mature career jumper, the sitting-stepping ship has sailed. If you've ever met this dog, you know his M.O. He is the bulldozer who will plow over you without missing a beat. It's time for the (not so) heavy artillery. I am embarrassed to admit this, but after having tried every technique and contraption to come down the pike over the past twenty-three years, I've yet to find a more effective, albeit unsophisticated, way to stop the jumping junkie than the old can of coins. I have even dressed it up and created the No Can Do, your problem-solving kit in a can. Here's a new spin on an old standby:

Select a heavy, all-metal can that has no other use in your household. Our goal is for the puppy to avoid the can, so you don't want him to freak every time you take a sip of your Schlitz. Decorative cans work well. Place twenty pennies in it and secure the lid. Leave the can strategically situated where Rover is most apt to jump on you and shake it just once midjump while saying "No!" Put the can down and immediately redirect him nicely to SIT. "Good boy!" Don't involve your friends or kids in this project yet. Most dogs dislike the sound enough for the association to be a powerful one: Do not jump on whoever holds the can. Use it sparingly. To overuse the can runs the risk of desensitizing Rover to the sound. Two or three shakes are all he'll ever need. Now take the coins out. The empty can is as compelling a conditioned aversive as the loaded one was. Only use No Can Do with puppies older than six months, and never use it with an ultrasensitive dog, as it may be too startling.

### INVOLVING OTHERS

Leave the empty No Can Do outside the door when your neighbor comes over for tea. Simply ask her to carry it inside with her. Same thing with the kids; their holding the empty can should now be enough to dissuade jumping. If you like you can use multiple cans in multiple locations. Place one on the sofa you want to keep the muddy puppy off and leave another on the kitchen counter. Eventually the lid alone may be all that's needed to keep the puppy from jumping. While playing up SIT and keeping four on the floor as acceptable greetings, phase out the can over a six-week period.

Jumping is one of those nasty problems that sneaks up on you, like gaining a pound here and there: It seems innocent at first, but it can be overwhelming when full-blown. The ideal, then, is to nip the puppy's jumping in the bud while you Can Do.

## Quid Pro Quo

Who hasn't battled with her dog to get him to relinquish something he shouldn't have, whether it's a sock, a rock, goose poop, or Saran Wrap? And the more passionately you attempt to get the contraband away from Rover, the more aggressively he'll guard it. Object guarding is potentially quite dangerous for both you and your dog. The object he is guarding might hurt him, and the zeal with which he feels compelled to guard it may cause him to hurt you.

The quid pro quo program is meant to teach Rover that if he lets you have whatever is in his mouth he will be rewarded with something of equal or greater value. Whether he gives up something legal like a ball, or illegal like a pair of pantyhose, he gets the goods. No questions asked.

Here's what to do: Firmly hold a small, hard biscuit between your thumb and first finger and offer it to Rover. Once the cookie is in his

**77**

mouth but before he clamps down, calmly say DROP and pull it away. "Good boy!" Repeat this a few times, then say OKAY, TAKE IT, and let Rover eat the cookie.

After a number of repetitions, try the exact same setup, but then, rather than giving him the cookie, offer him something even better, perhaps a bite of Brie. Next ask Rover to drop the glove and give him a squeaky toy. If he drops the ball his reward is your throwing it again.

See how it works? Quid pro quo shows Rover that it's worth his while to drop what's in his mouth, whether he actually puts it down or simply lets you take it without argument. Not knowing what to expect makes it all the more fun. It's like gambling with a guaranteed good hand. Will I have a flush or a full house? And every once in a while— oops!—no goodie. That Rover wins often enough keeps him at the table. Vary the objects that you practice with, the location, and number of times you say DROP before giving him the goods so that he doesn't simply think he needs to drop a sock in the den three times before receiving a reward. Keep him guessing. If you are too predictable, clever Rover will quickly catch on and only drop for the cool stuff. Practice quid pro quo preventatively as you would CPR. These are both life-saving skills.

Was I ever glad that I had worked on this with my late, great mutt Monty. Once, while on our daily woods walk, Monty ran over to me with a used rubber in his mouth. And not the kind you put on your foot. Had I conveyed my revulsion by screaming DROP IT! chances are very good that he would have either run away from me in fear or swallowed the damn thing as threatened dogs often do. Instead, I calmly asked him to DROP IT then quickly picked up a stick and threw it for him to chase. And mercifully Monty did.

For dogs who are mild to moderate guarders—either puppies or dogs whose possessiveness is not (yet) dangerous—teaching abundance usually helps. Present Rover with a seemingly limitless supply of food, toys, or whatever else he's guarding. There's more where that came from. This is what I did with my half-starved, six-week-old puppy, Plain Jane, who I found in the New York City subway twenty-one years ago. P. J. was extremely suspicious around food. So, rather than offer her a full bowl of food, a veritable gold mine to guard, I threw an equivalent amount of dry kibble around the apartment throughout the day. Learning that food was plentiful, P. J. came to devalue individual

> **WARNING: Some dogs become overstimulated by the abundance and their protectiveness is exacerbated rather than diminished. Remember, nothing works with all dogs, so here, as always, use your judgment and err on the side of safety.**

pieces and considered them hardly worth worrying about at all. After about ten days it was time to reintroduce the bowl.

Whatever your dog's background, food bowl guarding is quite common. Try the following from day one to prevent a problem later on. A dog cannot guard something that isn't his, so you maintain possession of the bowl by holding on to it while Rover chomps away. Your presence, and more specifically your hand, makes food happen. Sit on a chair next to him rather than hovering over him as this may be too threatening. Every once in a while, gently say DROP (or "leave it," "out," "trade"—it doesn't matter) and take the bowl away. Add an extraspecial goodie—chicken, cheese, a dollar bill—tell him OKAY and allow Rover to finish eating uninterrupted.

Once Rover's possessiveness has been diffused this way, put the bowl down before saying DROP midmeal. Again, remove the bowl, sweeten the pot, and let him eat on. Occasionally walk by eating Rover and toss him something scrumptious. "Wow! Dinner's even better when Ma's near by." Best not try this with young kids unless you are supervising. Some dogs actually guard the bowl itself or its location. Mix things up by using a plastic bowl one meal, metal another, and ceramic the third, offered in the kitchen, the laundry room, etc. Following these techniques for about ten to fourteen meals, which need not be consecutive, should be enough. Intermittent spot checks thereafter wouldn't hurt.

For some poor souls—usually dogs that came from puppy mills, lived on the streets, or were previously deprived—the primal need to guard limited resources runs very deep. For them, a squished worm might as well be a side of beef. The imprint of starvation may be impossible to erase. The same is true with people. I will never forget an affluent client whose nine-year-old Korean daughter, adopted from the streets of Seoul at age five, still stashed discarded food scraps under her canopy bed "just in case." Where there has been such profound depri-

**79**

vation, teaching your dog quid pro quo is probably too dangerous. I'd recommend seeking professional help.

Let me mention a few other warnings while I'm at it. First, it is not practical, or becoming, to argue with Rover over every single twig, scrap of paper, or blade of grass that he chews. Most dogs' digestive tracts process these things remarkably well.

I had a client—I'll call her Cruella—with a gentle, newly adopted shelter dog, Oliver. He had been a stray and was quite timid. Oliver once picked up a gum wrapper and Cruella went after him with such ferocity in an attempt to get it away from him that he nailed her. She shamelessly told me how she wouldn't let him "get away with stealing things" so she had him "destroyed." "If he'd bite over a piece of paper, what would he do with something that mattered?"

What she, a psychotherapist, didn't get was that as a street dog, Oliver had finely tuned survival skills. That wrapper mattered to him. Dogs, like all beings, have three possible responses to feeling threatened: flight, fight, or freeze. These are laws. By her own admission, she had yelled at Oli to drop the paper—something he may well have done had he ever been taught to—and when he didn't, she ran after him so that he fled to the bathroom. Cornered, he stood still, head lowered, yet Cruella kept coming. Because flight and freeze hadn't worked, all that was left for him to do was to fight. So Oliver bit her finger that wagged menacingly in his face. Damn, I'd have bitten her too. This sensitive dog had survived on the streets for who knows how long and then was killed two weeks later over a gum wrapper. This was a battle that should have never been picked.

Second, you should consider that if Rover absolutely refuses to relinquish something that you must get away from him, it pays to have an emergency plan. Let's say it is time to bring him inside and he's guarding a decomposed squirrel. Or a live rat. (He's a dog—it happens.) Water works wonders here. Spray water in Rover's face, which will (hopefully) disorient him enough to make him drop the rodent. Sashay him inside and (hopefully find someone else to) deal with the squirrel later.

Even worse, what if Rover steals a steak knife off the counter or a hunk of the broken mayonnaise jar? These things happen all the time. Obviously, you'll cut your hand if you grab it, so use tongs to hold the blade and squirt a little lemon juice or spray club soda from a shaken bottle into Rover's mouth to make him drop it.

Although these two simple strategies are not especially glamorous, they could save your dog's life. Water, lemon juice, club soda: How easy and safe is that? Much like having a fire extinguisher in the house, it pays to be prepared. I would recommend now revisiting quid pro quo (page 77).

## Nuisance Barking

Dogs bark for different reasons. There is a play bark, a territorial bark, an alarm bark, a fear bark, a predatory bark, a bored bark, and a bossy bark. Some dogs are even multilingual. Barking per se is not a problem. You'll be thrilled old Rover is on the case if a burglar's about. It is excessive barking that will make you and your neighbors nuts. Our goal, therefore, is to limit barking, not eliminate it.

Certain breeds bark way more than others. Terriers tend to be very opinionated. Your herders have a lot to say. And hounds love to tell the vermin they're a comin'. Since you don't know how vocal your dog will become—even the mildest puppy may become outspoken when grown up—the ideal time to teach QUIET is when he's still young.

QUIET only makes sense in the context of barking. For now, allow your barking pup to spontaneously stop and nicely say QUIET after the last bark. If protective barking is something you want to encourage, let old Rover know you're pleased he's on patrol by first saying, "Good boy," then QUIET. Now change the subject; SIT, "Brilliant boy!" Offer a cookie, take him for a walk, or give him dinner. The point is to demonstrate that good things follow being QUIET.

Keep this up for seven to ten days. "Woof, woof, woof, woof." QUIET. "Yeah, Rover!" "Woof, woof." QUIET. "Woof, woof, woof." QUIET. "Dang! Every time I stop barking Ma says QUIET. What are the odds?" Now that he's beginning to make the connection, it is time to turn it around. After an acceptable number of barks (10 to 20 seconds' worth) say QUIET. Offer him kudos for complying. Keep this up until QUIET is a cool game.

You might even enlist an accomplice to ring the doorbell, honk the horn, or do whatever will elicit barking to give you multiple opportunities to practice. Or you could try the following: Ring the bell and say SPEAK upon his beginning to bark. Bravo! Once he knows what SPEAK means, say, NO! SPEAK to silence him. Could you die?

I know, I know. I smell the skeptics among you. And you're right. Although these techniques are highly effective when taught to a budding barker, a more seasoned one will laugh in the face of QUIET and NO! SPEAK. Since behaviors strengthen with reinforcement, old Rover must have found barking to be richly rewarding for some time to become a nuisance barker in the first place. When QUIETdoesn't cut it, managing his barking may be the best you can hope for. Here are some suggestions:

The territorial barker woofs away the mailman six days a week. Mix in Mr. FedEx, the paperboy with a UPS chaser, and this cocktail of retreating trespassers reinforces his status as sentry dozens of times a month. Then, of course, you've got your joggers, bicyclists, and dog walkers. That all these interlopers would have left without Rover ever having barked never even occurs to him. He made them go. As the environment rewards the behavior, use the environment to prevent it. Something as simple as blocking his view of the intruders with drapes or bushes or using a gate to prevent his access to the picture window may be all that's needed.

A mild aversive like spraying your barker in the face with cold water from a plant mister is effective if he's sounding off in close proximity to you, for example while the two of you are in the car. Say QUIET as you spray in hopes that soon saying QUIET alone will work sans saturating the seat. It's best to know your audience here. Spritz a greyhound and he'll never bark for the rest of his natural life; spray a Portuguese water dog and he'll simply bark on.

Although I understand that tethering a dog may be a necessary short-term containment measure, to do so long-term may cause many safety and behavioral problems, one of which is frustration barking. I am a fan of fenced-in yards, but to leave Rover locked out all the time begs the question, "Why get a dog in the first place?" Often people intend for their puppy to be a house dog, but then they neglect to teach him the basics that would enable his inclusion in family life. The poor soul gets relegated to the backyard 24/7. Lonely and bored, the puppy becomes a barker. What else is there to do?

Dogs are highly social animals, and to isolate one is an invitation for trouble. Although a second dog will lessen the loneliness—and Lord knows I'm all for that—it may also double the barking. Pet dogs were bred to interact with people. That's why they're not cats. Most dogs I know would be happier cuddled up with you on the front seat of a sedan than home alone on an estate.

It obviously would have been preferable to address problem barking while the pup was young, but it is never too late. Of course you have a life and Rover's got to learn to tolerate time alone. My own dogs are home alone more than I'd like. The point is to stimulate him through play, exercise, and training when you can so that he's satisfied and tired (and therefore quiet) when you can't.

Predatory barking goes deep. This and play barking between dogs are something you have to learn to manage or live with. Try changing the subject to distract them.

Excessive play barking directed at you is bossy barking and needs to be extinguished (more on this in the Bossy Dog section on pages 96–99).

Not all dogs express their fearfulness through barking, but if yours does, follow the same desensitization and counterconditioning protocol recommended in the Timid Dog section on pages 93–96.

There are a number of antibarking collars and handheld devices on the market. The only time to consider using one of these is if the previous suggestions have failed. Here's the poop on some:

The collars fall into two categories: One group is (supposedly) activated by the vibration of the barking dog's vocal chords; the other has a remote control that enables you to determine when the correction is delivered. In each group there is one collar that emits a noise, another sprays citronella oil in the barking dog's face, and a third shocks him. Ethically, I don't have a problem with the sound collars. However, I've not found them to be terribly effective. The citronella collars work quite well for some barkers. Its main downside is a goopy, albeit bug-free, dog. I hate the shock collars. I've heard of many malfunctioning and zapping the hapless pup for scratching his neck or for saying "Hey" to his people. And though there are sophisticated time-delay options built into some, the collar doesn't discriminate between nuisance and appropriate barking. In my experience many people who rush to use shock collars have their own issues that should be worked out elsewhere. Under the most extreme of circumstances, I have recommended the use of this collar. I worked with a quadriplegic woman in assisted housing whose American Eskimo dog's barking was unacceptable. Moving was not an option for my client, nor was giving away her dog. As (relatively) justified as I felt using an antibark collar, having exhausted all other options, seeing the dog cringe upon receiving a shock broke my heart.

There are a few handheld devices that make a sound that interrupts the barking. These can be quite effective when well timed. Shaking No Can Do if Rover's near or tossing it to coincide with where he's sounding off—as though God dropped it—may do the trick.

I hope you realize that using aversives simply treats the symptoms. Unless the underlying cause of his barking is addressed, it will manifest elsewhere. So if yours is a bored barker and you deny him vocalizing without otherwise enriching his lot, he may take to digging up the yard or self-mutilation.

## Entrapment

My beloved puppy Buddha, a Bernese mountain dog/Australian shepherd mix, had the annoying habit of stealing tissues out of the bathroom garbage and shredding them into scores of gooey little globs. Why so many puppies adore doing this is beyond me. The only thing better for Buddha would have been my running after her in mad pursuit of the Kleenex; knowing that it would have brought about a chase may have motivated Buddha to steal tissues in the future. If left to her own devices, my Bu would also devour paper towels, toilet paper, napkins, you name it. I once caught her chomping on an installed roll of Scott Tissue as though it were an apple.

Because I believe it is vital to build up a puppy's confidence as much as possible for their first six months, I simply managed young Buddha by using gates and a crate, closing doors, and removing the garbage. It was my responsibility as her caretaker to prevent her having access to items of great danger to her or irreplaceable value to me. She was a baby, after all, and as such required adult supervision.

When Buddha was old enough I corrected her verbally and immediately redirected her to chew one of her toys when I caught her stealing a tissue. This taught Bu not to steal tissues in front of me. So she simply waited for me to leave the room to have at them.

To avoid this person present/person absent training trap, environmental conditioning comes into play. This simply means that the learning comes from the thing itself, the source. I let the garbage teach Buddha what to do. Here's how:

### THE STING

All I needed was three things: tissues, a prized toy, and a chewing aversive like Bitter Apple. To set up poor Bu, I threw a number of scrunched tissues in the trash, the funkier the better. Then I strategically placed her favorite fuzzy bunny next to it. Finally I spritzed the tissue with Bitter Apple and left the room.

My goal was to have Buddha's attempts to steal the tissue be foiled by its own foul taste and for her to choose to chew her bunny instead. And it worked. The operative word is "choose." She was in control of the consequences. Typically, five consecutive days is all it takes for even the most tenacious puppy to get that tissues are bad and dog toys are good. I simply left the Bitter Apple and a few cool toys in the bathroom and refreshed the setup every time I was in there. It took only seconds out of my day, and the best part is that my relationship with Bu is intact. Why should I be the bad guy when the Kleenex can? This, of course, works equally well with all manner of contraband no matter the pup's palate: socks, throw rugs, feminine hygiene products—give it a whirl.

Stealing tissues, of course, is a minor infraction. Recently, Buddha's thievery could have killed her. Now that she's over a year old I had relaxed her supervision in a way that had proven appropriate with other puppies. What I didn't fully appreciate was the compulsiveness of her stealing. I can only speculate that it is tied to her having been abandoned at just three weeks old at the shelter from which I adopted her. Mother issues, no doubt. Although I was still puppy-proofing obvious temptations in the house, I never thought that an unopened bottle of glucosamine/chondroitin for Stinky's arthritis posed a risk. Unbeknownst to me, Buddha stole the bottle off the kitchen counter, took it outside, tore into it, and ate all 120 pills while I was working on the computer. Later, at 2:45 A.M., she frantically woke me right before her projectile diarrhea exploded all over my bedroom walls. We rushed to the all-night emergency vet, where she stayed for two days and $700 worth of treatment. She is now fine. And very agile. But this event was a wake-up call that despite thinking I had taught Buddha how to behave in the kitchen, we had a serious problem that required intensive intervention.

## STING NUMBER TWO: THE BAGEL BOPPER

This time the correction needed to come from the counter. Enter the "Bagel Bopper," one of No Can Do's many variations. All you need to make a bopper is a bagel (duh), twenty pennies, a heavy metal can, and string. Place the coins in the can, secure the lid, and then tie one end of the string to the can and the other to the bagel (dabbing a little cream cheese on the bagel wouldn't hurt). Put the bagel at the counter's edge with the can set back about a foot, and then leave the room. As with all covert operations, the subject must not see the setup.

The goal here was for Buddha to surreptitiously steal the bagel and in so doing cause the can to come crashing down and startle her. And she did. As if on cue, Bu grabbed the bagel that very first night. The can of pennies never touched her, but the noise alone was enough to do the trick. Sound aversives can be very powerful while doing no real damage. I repeated the setup for five consecutive days on different surfaces throughout the kitchen with cheese, chicken, a sponge, and a peanut-filled pill bottle as bait. It's been about a month now, and though I still don't trust her fully, it only took that one episode for Buddha to catch on. As young puppies require close supervision, this technique should clearly only be used with those at least six months old.

When policing and mild aversives fail, a Scat Mat, which emits a low-level shock when stepped on, almost always works. I hate going this route, but if using one had been necessary to keep Buddha safe, I would have.

I got lucky with Buddha in that the Bagel Bopper did the trick. However, beware the crafty canine who simply eats the bagel without pulling it. This, of course, would encourage, not discourage, jumping on the counter. That's exactly what happened with the boxer Tyson. His person, Wendy, is a food stylist, so there is always fabulous food about. While at Wendy's house, I reached for the box of tissues in anticipation of a sneeze, which caused Tyson to run out of the room. This, apparently, was his normal response. We decided to exploit this discovery by perching the tissue box at the counter's edge. The box has kept him off the counters for four months now. Go figure.

With all material reinforcers, whether positive or negative, the goal is to become independent of them quickly. Although there is nothing wrong with leaving an attractive tissue box or No Can Do on the kitchen counter, the point is for your dog to learn not to jump, not to simply avoid the box.

Finally, I have learned over the years how uncommon common sense can be, so forgive me for stating the obvious. If you have a large dog, do not leave thawing meat or a bowl of Halloween candy on the kitchen counter, as chocolate can be deadly to dogs. I got a call Easter Sunday from a hysterical client whose black Labrador, Corian, ate eight solid chocolate bunnies—foil and all—and the ham that was intended to feed twelve. How did the dog have time to eat everything? Despite my having been hired specifically to curb Corian's counter cruising, the dog was left locked in the kitchen with the ham cooling on the counter while the family went to church. *Hello!* The woman isn't stupid— she's a district attorney—she "just didn't think." I hear this all the time.

Similarly, when I was ten, my family had a collie, Lady, who we believed was Lassie incarnate. In my family's eyes, Lady could do no wrong. We came home one night to what looked like a murder scene. Blood was splattered throughout the house and pools of it were congealing on the kitchen floor. Lady had knocked over a strawberry shortcake on a glass platter and in the process of devouring the cake had cut her mouth and a foot on the broken glass. Perplexed, my father questioned the veterinarian as to how our perfect pet could have done such a thing. "She's a dog," the vet said, "and don't ever forget it."

## On Being Alpha'ed Out

An inviolable law of dog training is never, *ever* let your dog sleep on your bed. While I'd never actually prescribe it, for lots of us it's a cozy time we enjoy spending with our dogs that we would hate to give up. At least once a week a client confesses to me that she allows her dog to sleep on the bed. So seeing as there are so many of you out there seeking absolution, I figure it's worth addressing.

Gritty sheets and hairy pillows aside, there is one serious reason why some dogs should be banned from the bed: biting. A dog with a heightened startle response may lash out reflexively when awakened. Another, vying for dominance, might view your passivity in bed as a chance to make a power play. But just because some dogs are unreliable,

87

why ban them all? It's like denying all children ice cream because a few are lactose intolerant.

The notion of alpha—or "top dog" à la wolf society—is very popular these days. Many dog trainers, veterinarians, and others obsessed being alpha staunchly perpetuate the idea that dogs should not sleep on the bed. To be alpha, they maintain, it is best to have your beast sleep beneath you. Show him who's boss. Having studied wolves for more than twenty years, I assure you that the alphas sleep amid their lower-ranking pack members.

Two of the other rules the alpha obsessed insist upon—and there are many—is having your dog eat after you and follow you out of doors. You're the leader after all! Theoretically, this is sound enough. However, if I, a dog-savvy single person, find this virtually impossible to institute, I have to challenge the practicality of this doctrine in an active household where everyone is eating and exiting all day long. Wolves are born into this caste system. And unless we are also encouraged to scent mark and wag our tails, I think it's best we not mix our metaphors.

If you are still intent on Rover sleeping on your bed, I'd recommend the following: Have a designated sheet, towel, or blanket that you condition your dog to lie down on. This can most easily be accomplished by placing the blanket where you know from experience he likes to sleep. As he begins to lie down, assign words to it; "on the blanket" will do. You can make the blanket extra-attractive by sitting on it yourself.

After about five days, put the blanket on your bed and invite Rover on up. Pat it while saying "on the blanket." Next place the blanket on the floor and with equal enthusiasm encourage Rover "on the blanket." "Yeah, Rover!" On the bed. Off the bed. On the bed. Off the bed. Where the blanket is, he can sleep. The ability to get Rover off the bed easily will not only do wonders for your love life, it will also come in handy should Rover become disabled.

A few years ago Stinky, my rottweiler/German shepherd cross who had always slept on my bed, had double cruciate ligament surgery. Prior to the surgery I played up the "off the bed" piece so that when he came home all bandaged and gimpy he knew to go straight onto his blanket on the floor. Using a blanket is also useful if you travel with

Rover or need to board him. If you have conditioned him to sleep wherever the blanket is, the security blanket's presence will ease his transition into the new digs.

## Can You Dig It?

Dogs dig. It's what they do. *That* they dig is a given over which we have zero control. Our objective is to understand *why* they dig so we can teach them *where* we want them to do it.

Why do dogs dig?

- To unearth cooler dirt on a hot day

- To pursue moles, worms, or other critters

- To relieve boredom

- To bury a bone

If your dog digs for the first reason, providing a hard plastic kiddy pool on hot days may be all that's needed. My Buddha is very proud of her "above ground." Unfortunately for those whose dogs dig for the second reason, there is no way to teach a dog not to pursue vermin that nest in your lawn. For dachshunds and terriers, in particular, this is their raison d'être. Sorry. Best get rid of the rodents. Boredom is the main reason that dogs dig. As with the bored barker (see page 81), enriching Rover's environment is the key to solving the problem. Bone burying, on the other hand, is a basic canid behavior. Aside from not giving Rover bones, the only way around his destroying your yard is to teach him where to bury them. Try the following with all digging dogs.

Select an innocuous Designated Dig Spot (DDS) that is both aesthetically acceptable and safe, such as under a bush or behind the garage. Some people even try a sandbox. Have a trowel and marrow or other dog-safe bone handy. Make a big deal out of marching over to the DDS, dig a hole, place the bone in it, and push the dirt back over it. As your dog begins to dig up the newly buried bone—and he will—hoot and holler "Yeah, Rover! This is where a good dog digs." There's no need to call him over or to purposefully engage him in the process. A little mystery adds to the fun. Repeat this two or three times and

**89**

then quit for the day. Remove the bone. Practice this for about five days, playing up the walking over to the DDS and emphasizing your code words "where a good dog digs."

Now, while supervising, anticipate your dog's desire to dig either to bury a bone or lie down, and in an upbeat voice ask, "Rover, where's a good dog dig?" Bravos abound if he marches on over to the DDS all on his own. I would love to tell you that all dogs get this and it works all the time. But it doesn't. However, it works often enough that it's well worth trying. Good luck.

## CHAPTER 7

# Special Needs

What to do if Rover is desperately shy, pushes you around, or can't stand to be left alone.

**I miss you already!**

B
ehavior is a blend of nature and nurture. We are all born with genetic predispositions, which, if fostered, result in the expression of that trait. So, if a child born with musical tendencies is offered piano lessons, her talent has the potential to be fully realized. If, on the other hand, she is predisposed to cry a lot and that tendency is indulged, you sure wouldn't want to sit next to her on an airplane.

Whether or not music or crying is actually encouraged, these predispositions still exist just below the surface, ready to emerge. This is the challenge of influencing a dog's behavior; you want to accentuate the positive traits while thwarting the undesirable ones. It is a balancing act requiring constant adjustments.

## The Timid Dog

Nowhere is the challenge of shaping a dog's behavior greater than with timid dogs. Some dogs are born timid and others are made that way by abusive handling. And because fear is the main reason dogs bite, there is no greater nature/nurture nightmare than a genetically timid dog who has been abused. This poor soul is an accident waiting to happen.

No person or puppy is confident in every context, but the clinically timid dog goes beyond shy and appears desperate, almost paranoid. This is the puppy in the litter that holds back. He's the least likely to approach new people and may be reluctant to explore novel things. His fearfulness interferes with his enjoyment of life and, often, our enjoyment of him. People are often attracted to him when selecting a puppy, either because they feel sorry for him or because they believe he'll be a laid-back adult. Charming though he may be, I would discourage families with young children from taking a timid puppy.

For many of us who are committed to adopting dogs out of shelters and those in need of a home, timidity is a common problem. Rehabilitating these dogs is a painstaking process and is clearly not for everyone. It can be extremely gratifying, however, for those who are up to it. No matter what the puppy is afraid of and to what degree, the remedy is the same. He needs to be systematically desensitized to the object(s) of fear while concurrently counterconditioned that good things happen in their presence. The variables are the speed with which you proceed, how far you can go, and how long it will take to get there.

When I am hired to help with a timid dog, I will typically ignore him at first and quickly sit down. The main mistake well-intentioned people make with these dogs is to come on too strong too fast. This can do more harm than good. Rover needs to make the first move. Sitting makes me less threatening than standing. Timid dogs appreciate this. First sessions are often awkward because my client is paying me beaucoup bucks and I am completely ignoring my charge.

Food is a powerful icebreaker with timid dogs. It is vital that the delivery of food be well timed. Once Rover settles down, typically far away from me, I'll toss treats underhand his way. To try to sweet-talk him out of the corner he's cowering in is too much pressure for our first date. It's a good sign if Rover eats the treats. I have seen emaciated dogs refuse food because their fear trumped their hunger. Should he be relaxed enough to approach me, I'll offer food from my hand held at his chest level. Where it gets dicey is if the pup is threatening—growling, snarling, or lunging. I withhold treats in this case lest he misinterpret these behaviors as a means of getting food. It is important to acknowledge his *actions,* not his *attitude.* Cowering and lunging are flip-side expressions of Rover's fear. His objective is to maximize the distance between us, either by retreating himself or by causing me to retreat. Avoiding me is a reinforceable choice for our first meeting. Menacing me is not.

Try leaving a lightweight leash on Rover, inside or out. This is a confidence builder for many dogs, even if no one is holding on to it. The lead suggests that someone else is in charge and that he will be taken care of. Using a leash could be counterproductive, however, should Rover have a prior negative association with it. To hook the lead on him and then not go for a walk is a tease, so take Rover out and then simply "forget" to take the lead off. Clearly, only leave it on him when you are home, awake, and supervising. And never use a choke chain.

An added practical advantage of his dragging the leash around is that it gives you something to step on or grab should you need to intervene. A stressed dog may perceive your hand reaching for his collar as a threat and bite it, whereas I have never seen a dog lash out at a foot stepping on the leash. It's as though it is somehow separate from you.

Once Rover begins to relax, it's time to raise the bar by rewarding progressively more confident displays. In this case this means his tolerating less distance between the two of us. Let's say Rover has established a comfort zone of ten feet. Although I'd prefer he make the overture and advance toward me, even if he doesn't, I will still reinforce his tolerating my advancing to nine or nine-and-a-half feet.

We're talking baby steps here. Consider all gained ground a victory and quit while you're ahead. The next session will start at this newly established level of confidence. There will be advances and setbacks. Such is the nature of behavior. So long as there is more progress than steps backward, the program is working. If the puppy regresses, I split the difference by backing off a little, but perhaps not quite as much as Rover would want.

## A TRICK THAT WORKS WONDERS

It's hard to act relaxed when you're tense, to not show fear when you are afraid. If you find that Rover's behavior makes projecting a calm, confident demeanor difficult, try singing. Yes, singing. Anxiety that is communicated through the spoken voice often isn't apparent when we sing. And did you know that people who stutter can sing without stammering? Apparently, a different part of the brain is engaged. I also suspect that the joyfulness of singing overrides one's insecurities. So, the next time Rover makes you uneasy, sing him a little ditty. I know you feel like an idiot. Here's hoping no one is listening.

95

Sitting perpendicular to Rover diffuses the intensity of a face-to-face confrontation. My voice is friendly, my eyes are soft, my hand gestures are small, and my posture is confident (to be tentative with a timid dog keeps him on guard). I always reach under, not over, his head. Engage Rover in activities you've learned he enjoys, such as walking or retrieving. This will not only cause him to associate positive things with you, but it will also take his mind off his insecurities.

I have had great success using clickers with timid dogs. Once Rover has been primed to associate clicks with treats, try clicking as a way of telling him what a big, brave boy he is. The beauty part is that strangers have the exact same click as you. Aside from marking the specific behavior you wish to reinforce, the clicking sound itself can actually elevate your dog's spirits, much like a song might lift yours.

It is important to have realistic expectations for bashful Rover. He may never be the life of the party. Sometimes the best we can hope for is a compromise that is safe and mutually acceptable. For example, my Monty was uneasy around loud little boys. I didn't have any myself, but when one came over for a visit, Monty and I agreed that he could avoid the child by quietly retreating into the bedroom. It would have been wonderful had he actually come to enjoy their company, but in lieu of that, the two of us managed very nicely for eleven years.

## The Bossy Dog

This is the dog who looks you squarely in the eyes and barks, "Yo! Walk me. Feed me. Rub me. Throw me a toy." Me, me, me! In a restaurant he'd be the fool snapping his fingers in the busboy's face to demand more bread. And he always has to have the last word. Dog owners—and a lot of professionals for that matter—label him "dominant" or "alpha." I call him bossy.

The terms "alpha" and "dominant" get bandied about a lot these days, often erroneously. So far this week I have received eight calls from people claiming to have an "alpha dog." One was even alleged to be "ultra-alpha." But to label is to limit and runs the risk of sending us in the wrong direction. Behavior is rarely so simple. People who never say "No" can make any dog bossy, whatever his genetic predisposition.

Hierarchies exist in all societies; this maintains order. The truly alpha dog doesn't need to bully; he's a natural leader. There is no need for Michael Jordan to scream, "I'm the best," he just is. It is typically the beta, or second string, who has to prove himself. I have worked with many celebrities who were totally respectful and genuine, while their employees were ever so full of themselves.

Blended households—dog/human—have to establish human rules that dogs can live with. These are non-negotiable. The bossy dog emerges by repeatedly getting his way for bending these rules. Here's what I mean: Let's say baby Rover is restless. You think he has to pee, so you rush him outside. Fair enough. Or, convinced that he's famished, you feed him. But what if Rover just emptied himself ten minutes earlier and it's still two hours until lunch? He might just *want* to go out and play in the snow. Some dogs always seem hungry; it doesn't mean they *need* to eat. I would have loved to have eaten that whole crumb cake this morning but ... Sometimes, you just have to say "No!" True, you do run the risk of Rover having an accident by not snapping to and rushing him out each and every time he demands. To which I say, "So what?" It's urine, not uranium. You are occasionally going to misinterpret Rover's signals; we all do. It is better to have to wipe up the ill-placed puddle than to always give in and create a monster you won't want to live with. Your bossy dog might bite you.

I was sitting at a client's kitchen table recently discussing the circumstances surrounding her two-year-old, 110 pound Rhodesian ridgeback's having seriously bitten her twice. The woman needed reconstructive surgery after the second bite. Patty got up from the table twelve times in thirty minutes to let Zambia in and out. It was obviously a well-established routine. When I asked her about this, my soft-spoken client said she didn't want Zambia to lift his leg inside, as he'd taken to doing. Also, Patty's husband was on her case because the dog had scratched the newly painted door. Zambia had Patty well trained to jump.

Here's what I recommended: First, have Zambia neutered. An intact male is more macho and apt to mark his territory by lifting his leg than one who is neutered. Studies have shown that neutering at any age is 80 percent effective behaviorally. Next, we taught Zambia the basic obedience exercises outlined earlier. This is the armature upon which a more substantial relationship can be built. Dogs do not bite people they respect. As expected, Zambia was especially resistant to the DOWN STAY, but we worked him through it. Then, Patty put Zam-

"But his tail was wagging"

In describing the circumstances leading up to Rover's biting, all too often I am told, "His tail was wagging." The tail wag is an extremely ambiguous piece of body language. Yes, the sweeping, horizontal wag is a happy, friendly sign but did you know that an upright tail wag could be a dominant display while a low wag is a sign of submission? A rapid wag represents arousal and a slow, low wag suggests uncertainty. And what about dogs whose tails are docked or the perpetually rigid, erect tail of many terriers? Hunting dogs wag ecstatically as they catch and kill their prey just as the tracker does upon cornering his quarry.

Because the tail wag is so easily misinterpreted, in assessing a dog's approachability, look for an overall relaxed demeanor—mouth, eyes, ears and hackles—in addition to a wiggling rear end. When in doubt, don't touch.

bia on the "No Free Lunch" program. This meant he needed to SIT, LIE DOWN, or otherwise earn food, toys, and being let in and out. "No Free Lunch" had to be strictly enforced for six weeks, then more casually followed for the rest of his life.

Given his naturally dominant nature and the degree to which Zambia was accustomed to getting his way, he predictably challenged Patty's every effort to assert herself. Here I suggested Patty do "the De Niro." Rather than backing off, she needed to step forward and say, "You talkin' to me?" Nothing deflates a bully better than being unbullyable (I believe that's from the Latin). Dogs are keenly sensitive to interpersonal space. Whoever retreats is viewed as acquiescing to the other's advances. This is how a Border collie can manage so many sheep. The dog controls the space. Patty, therefore, had to reclaim her home by never allowing Zambia to back her up. There is no democracy in dogdom. If Patty wasn't in charge, Zambia would be.

The only way to stop Zambia's pawing at the door was to ignore it. Remember, behaviors will be extinguished so long as they are not fanned with acknowledgment. I therefore recommended that they temporarily affix a piece of Plexiglas to the door and simply allow him to have at it. My prediction was that it would take ten days for Zambia to figure out that sitting at the back door, not scratching, would get it to open.

It is too soon to tell how well this plan has worked, the variable being Patty's ability to stay the course. Hopefully, I impressed upon her that she had to succeed at every level. To give in to any of Zambia's demands would only make matters worse. With a dog that outweighed her, that could prove catastrophic. For safety's sake, when dealing with a dangerous dog, I strongly recommend that you seek professional help.

## The Lonely Dog

Dogs hate being alone. As highly social pack animals, aloneness is not natural for them. That so many dogs accept solitude is more remarkable to me than that some do not. Full-blown separation anxiety goes way beyond Rover's missing you, it is a desperate state for your poor creature, and living with him can try the patience of even the most devoted of dog people.

Typically, dogs with separation anxiety are gentle souls who are calm when with us and totally out of control when left alone. How each dog acts out is an expression of his own predisposition, much like one anxious person overeats, another drinks, and a third buys shoes. One dog may bark nonstop all day; another chews absolutely everything; and a third, who's otherwise housebroken, pees and poops uncontrollably. There is often evidence of their frantic attempts to escape, such as downed drapes and scratched exit doors. Indeed, many do escape. I've known truly phobic dogs to jump out windows and chew through walls. Many develop separation anxiety anorexia. Some introverted dogs even self-mutilate. Lonely Doberman pinschers are known for this.

I became a dog trainer because of one such dog, Mowgli, a magnificent Belgian sheepdog/malamute mix I found on the Upper West Side of Manhattan twenty-four years ago. I routinely saw Mowgli dodging traffic while out walking my German shepherd Algunza. (It was supposed to be Aldonza from *Man of La Mancha*, but I mispronounced it.)

We were in the midst of a record-breaking heat wave. A network of West Side dog walkers and I had been tracking this terrified dog for weeks. No one could get near him. Finally, in a dehydrated stupor, Mowgli collapsed, enabling us to catch him. As all the other dog walkers came up with better—or at least faster—excuses than I as to why they couldn't take him home, I begrudgingly agreed to take him for "just one day."

I must have been nuts, or perhaps I didn't want to allow myself to care for this difficult dog, but I went out for dinner that first night. When I returned home a scant two hours later, Mowgli was waiting for me in the lobby. He had chewed his way out of my apartment, descended four flights of stairs, and, despite ample opportunity to escape, waited for me to return. That sealed our fate. Mowgli and I were together for the next twelve years. Rehabilitating Mowgli by the seat of my pants was so satisfying that I decided to pursue doing it for a living.

Although any dog can develop separation anxiety, those most at risk, like Mowgli, have been lost or abandoned. Not all abandoned dogs have this problem, of course. My Algunza was pregnant and visibly abused when I found her, yet she was fine.

It is quite common for dogs adopted into the best, most loving of homes from the worst, most abusive of backgrounds to develop separation anxiety. This apparent paradox is typically difficult for his adoptive family to accept. Some people even feel hurt, unappreciated: "We love him so much. Shouldn't he feel more, not less, secure with us?"

Here's how I understand it: Let's say you used to rent a dumpy old basement apartment with hand-me-down furniture and you finally bought and furnished your first home. Although you may not have even locked the apartment doors, you now install an alarm system. You've got more to lose. So it is with your dog's new digs. (A word on anthropomorphism: To anthropomorphize is to do dogs a disservice. I only use human analogies in hopes of helping you better understand your dog's behavior.)

**100**

Separation anxiety is unquestionably one of the most difficult of dog problems to deal with. As it only exists when we're not home, how are we supposed to fix it? A canine catch-22. And to make matters worse, its manifestations—chewing, barking, etc.—are all things dogs also do for other reasons. It is therefore easy to misinterpret Rover's misdeeds as poor training or—God forbid—spite. Those who make this mistake often express anger upon returning home to discover the dastardly deeds their dog did. This is 100 percent guaranteed to exacerbate the problem.

So what's a person to do? Because it is impossible to know which dogs will develop separation anxiety there are some preventative measures all new dog owners can take, no matter Rover's age or background, to minimize the chances of it developing. From day one, have the puppy spend some time alone. Even if you work at home or have taken time off to be with your new pup, which I encourage, he must see that you leave and, more importantly, that you return. It need not be for long; a few minutes a pop is enough for starters.

Of course, leave Rover in his crate or a cozy space that you've already acclimated him to. Hand him a favorite toy, give him a kiss, and calmly leave. It's okay for now if Rover fusses. He's a baby and they do that. After a few minutes, calmly return. Departures and arrivals are the tough times, like takeoffs and landings. Indeed, video cameras have shown that the first twenty minutes after you leave and the last twenty minutes before you return, should you be on a predictable schedule, are when most of Rover's acting out will occur. Anxious dogs whose people return home at random times may become undone upon hearing the garage or elevator door open or the key in the front door. Your goal, therefore, is to come and go, come and go, and in so doing downplay its significance. No big deal here.

It is essential that while you are always kind, you're also unemotional, almost aloof. Whether you are feeling sad, guilty, or nervous about leaving Rover, conveying your angst may actually legitimize his and set him up to respond in kind. Rover doesn't get that you are upset *for* him; he thinks you are upset *at* him. Ever notice how if you step on your dog's foot by accident he apologizes to you? He thought you did so because you were mad at him, not because you're a big old klutz. So if Rover believes that you're upset with him every time you leave, you are making the thing he most dreads—being alone—much worse.

The reason calm reunions are vital is twofold. First, if you are too manic when you return home, Rover's anticipation of this blessed event may be too much to bear and actually exaggerate his loneliness. The feast magnifies his perception of the famine. You are not the Messiah after all, so tone your arrival down.

What's worse, however, is to return home only to express anger at Rover's misdeeds. It is frustrating, I know, to be met by yet another pile of poop, but I promise you that your wrath will only elevate his anxiety and make matters worse for both of you. Poor Rover is emotionally overwrought, but your dispassionate demeanor can help neutralize his panic and actually anchor him. Enduring memories are those most associated with powerful emotions, both positive and negative. If the pup's on emotional overdrive, a composed response conveys that everything is okay.

Dogs with full-blown separation anxiety may require temporary support through using either a natural remedy or a prescription medication. Being holistically oriented, I would recommend first trying Rescue Remedy, a Bach Flower Remedy that can be bought in health food stores. I take Rescue Remedy, an all-natural product that calms, and I give it to all of my animals, including the birds, in times of stress. It is a subtle formula that takes the edge off Rover's anxiety so that he is more receptive to the behavioral work at hand. There are numerous other products, with which I am less familiar, marketed for dogs in natural food stores these days as well.

The FDA has also approved a drug called Clomicalm specifically for dogs with separation anxiety. Its protocol states that Clomicalm should be used in conjunction with a behavior-modification program so that the dog can be weaned off it once the desired results have been achieved. Because this drug can cause side effects, I believe its use is justified only in serious cases.

Whether or not you use either of these formulas, the following recommendations are the same:

1. A tired dog is less apt to be anxious, so make sure Rover's well exercised before leaving him home alone.

2. Feed Rover a low-protein diet to take a little of the oomph out of him.

3. If Rover paws at the closed door that contains him, try using a gate instead, if possible. Being able to see out seems to lessen many dogs' stress. If necessary you can place one gate on top of another.

4. As mentioned in Chapter 1, if the radio or TV is usually on when you are home, then leaving it on when you are out may

be soothing. Again, turning it on solely to keep Rover company may be counterproductive, as it will only serve to signal your departure.

5. Teaching STAY provides repeated opportunities for you to demonstrate that you return. As we all resist what we most need, dogs with separation anxiety have a hard time with this exercise. A dog's resistance here can actually be diagnostic of the disorder. And remember to say WAIT, not STAY, when you actually leave.

There are those who say that a dog's following you from room to room is a sure sign of separation anxiety. I disagree. Yes, anxious dogs do this, but so do many other, more balanced dogs. I mention it because I have heard of veterinarians who mistakenly prescribe Clomicalm based on this symptom alone. As this shadowing can be annoying no matter Rover's motivation, simply ignore his following you and reinforce his behavior when he does not. So, if you are finally able to go to the bathroom solo, make a big deal over Rover's having toughed it out alone when you return.

Meanwhile, it's time to begin counterconditioning Rover so that good things happen in your absence. Before leaving, hand him a long-lasting scrumptious something to chew. Remember to rub it, thereby marinating it with your scent. This could be a raw marrow bone or a makeshift one as described in the Chewing section (pages 35–38). Offer this in conjunction with the key tinkling. Once he's thoroughly

Dogs are masters at memorizing our predeparture rituals: We pick up our keys, put on our coats, arm the alarm, etc. This serves as an early warning system that puts the panic in motion. "Mayday! Ma's leaving. Pa's leaving. Mayday!" This is where your desensitization must begin. Pick up the keys, put down the keys. Pick up the keys, put down the keys. Keep it up until he learns the irrelevance of key lifting. Put your coat on, take your coat off. On, off. On, off. It's a bore, I know, but separation anxiety's tough.

into chewing the bone, casually say good-bye and leave. Ideally, stay out about twenty minutes. Come back calmly and remove the bone that will only reappear when you get ready to leave next time, thereby sweetening the sorrow of your departure.

With so profound a problem as separation anxiety, it typically takes at least six symptom-free weeks to trust that the behavior modification program has worked. Major changes like moving, illness, or kids returning to school at the end of the summer can cause regressions. A ten-day remedial touch-up is usually all Rover needs to recover. Good luck!

## CHAPTER 8

# Special Relationships

The addition of a new family member always requires adjustments and typically causes some stress. To minimize conflict, this chapter addresses how to best introduce a new dog into your and your existing dog's lives, as well as how to ensure that resident Rover accepts a newborn baby without incident.

105

## Getting a Second Dog

N ot since finding Mowgli roaming the Upper West Side of New York City twenty-four years ago have I lived with just one dog. Usually, there are three. Sometimes four. Although I treasured the intimacy I shared with Algunza, the German shepherd who came everywhere with me, I doubt I'll ever live with an only dog again. Observing the interplay between dogs is half the fun; the purity of it makes me feel free. September 11 wasn't that long ago. That day when we lost our innocence as a nation, my dogs played amongst themselves as joyfully as they had the day before.

The decision to take on a second dog is a big one. Only do so if *you* want two dogs. To acquire a second dog for the benefit of the first might backfire. I had a client, Jason, whose Norwegian elkhound, Houdini, scaled the six-foot chain-link fence to play with the Afghan next door. Jason installed an underground fence as a backup. So strong was Houdini's drive that he withstood the shock in addition to climbing the fence to get to his woman. Finally, in desperation, Jason adopted a second dog in hopes she'd keep the first one home. You guessed it. Rather than anchoring Houdini, Echo learned the ropes from the escape artist. Jason now has two disappearing dogs, one of whom he didn't really want.

**107**

Although I think multiple dogs are wonderful, taking on littermates, especially those of the same sex, can be tricky. Yes, they entertain each other, but, like human twins, they could bond so tightly that you will have a difficult time breaking in. Littermates of the same sex are even more inclined to fight than another same-sex pair. And then there's all that work: two sets of needle teeth chomping on your toes; twice the pee and poop to clean up; double-duty barking. People often think, "Well I'm tied down anyway with one, why not two?" Which makes sense conceptually, but puppies don't necessarily awaken, relieve themselves, and chew synchronously. And you don't know who did what when.

Whether you adopt an adult dog or a puppy, the ideal time to introduce the second is when the first is around two. By then you pretty much know the dog you're living with. Patterns are established; you finish each other's sentences. Selecting dogs of similar energy levels heightens compatibility. If you only intend to have two dogs, I'd recommend getting the opposite sex, as there is less chance of fighting.

Often people wait until too late in the first dog's life to introduce a second. Knowing that Rover's days are numbered, they want a puppy to ease the agony of the inevitable. I was just at a house with a fourteen-year-old shell of a wheaten terrier and a nine-week-old puppy. The poor old dog was tortured by the youngster, who was being yelled at by her people for doing what puppies do. The disparity of energy is comparable to that of an octogenarian and a toddler.

Introductions are important. Be prepared and act nonchalant. Have resident Rover well exercised before bringing the newcomer home and remove provocative objects (food bowls, bones, etc.). If you have previously visited Roverette, bring home something with her scent to leave with number one, and vice versa. Have number two's crate and other accessories in place for a few days and allow number one to investigate. I typically also add a few drops of Rescue Remedy to the drinking water prior to introductions.

If the newcomer is an adult dog, it is best to let them meet on neutral territory. Talk positively to each about the other. Allow them to check one another out thoroughly; some posturing is possible. Once they have sniffed one another, go for a walk and allow them to interact as much—or as little—as they choose. Then bring them home together.

Should you be getting a puppy, realize how overwhelming this day is for her. She just left her biological family and the only home and people she has ever known and may have traveled a great distance to get to you. It is important that she feel secure, so I'd recommend that you sit on the floor with her. Should the pup just want to sit on your lap while Rover number one gives her the once over, so be it. If she's bold enough to venture out, encourage her doing so while also sweet-talking number one. Be braced for a few anxious moments when Rover clobbers the puppy with his big old foot or snarls at the baby for overstepping boundaries. Within reason, allow this; it's how puppies learn. Junior was carried around in her mother's mouth and beaten up by littermates for weeks. She's hardier than you may think. Know that it is extremely rare for an adult dog to harm a puppy, though it could happen. Being relaxed here sets the tone for things to come. If the presence of the puppy stresses you, Rover will be less inclined to embrace her than if you communicate how happy you are she is here. As mentioned in the Timid Dog section (pages 93–96), this might be the perfect time to break into song.

Once you have introduced the puppy, keep Rover's routine intact. If he is used to going to the park at noon, take him. It doesn't matter that the puppy is too young to be included, and it's important that they are sometimes separated. The puppy will (hopefully) go to school and is in need of the same degree of socializing to a variety of people, places, and things as number one. This will accustom both to being home alone.

I am amazed by how many people worry that the pup will resent being crated if the adult is free. Don't. Dogs don't keep score. Would you worry about the baby's sleeping in a crib while her siblings are in beds? If number one is still crated, they should each have their own crate and be fed separately. Stealing each other's toys, roughhousing, and occasional disagreements are all to be expected. I'd recommend teaching them to take turns. Let's say you're grooming number one when the puppy pushes in. Calmly say, "It's Rover's turn," and continue brushing him. After thirty seconds, say, "Now it's the puppy's turn," and transfer your attention to her. This works equally well in blended households, with a dog and a cat, a dog and a bird, or a dog and a baby. Last night Murray Bird was on my shoulder and we were having a moment when Buddha butted in. I simply told her it was Murray's turn while I scratched his head. Bu lay down, sighed, and awaited her turn.

You may think that number one should be top dog by virtue of his seniority. And he may be. But dogs have their own hierarchies that they need to be allowed to work out. We tend to judge this by mistakenly placing a higher value on the alpha position and therefore penalize the newcomer's move to take over. Don't. To interfere here runs the risk of supporting one who is ill equipped to lead. Not everyone is cut out to be CEO; some dogs just need to work in the mailroom.

**109**

## Bringing Home Baby

I would recommend beginning to ready Rover for this blessed event at least two months before your due date. Envision the changes in Rover's routine that will be caused by the baby's arrival and start to institute them well before Junior comes home.

Change can cause stress and stress may cause regression. One dog might take up chewing again and another piddles in the living room while a third goes back to gambling. So if Rover is used to visiting the dog park twice a day but you only expect to have time to take him once daily after the baby arrives, slowly phase out one trip. I don't think it is wise to have him sleep on your bed with a newborn. Because your bed is the box seat of dog beds, work on Rover's demotion well in advance of the baby's birth so that he doesn't associate it with her (more in On Being Alpha'ed Out on pages 87–89). If you would like for him to go for walks with Junior and you (or, rather, for Junior to go for walks with you and Rover), practice HEEL with a doll in the carriage; it's best to iron out the logistics while it's safe to do so. If you haven't already done so, now's a good time to accustom Rover to wearing a Gentle Leader headcollar (page 62). Bone up on the DOWN STAY command; the longer Rover can stay down the better. This will enable Rover to be with the baby and you, but be out of the way. Practice in the actual locations you expect him to later hang out while you coo over the doll. If you have a friend with an infant, make a tape of baby sounds in order to familiarize Rover and play it while he's engaged in his favorite activities (there are commercial CDs and audiotapes available as well).

Once your baby is born and she's still in the hospital, Dad—or whoever—should bring home an item of the baby's to place on the doll. With the tape playing, allow Rover to scrutinize the surrogate while joyfully being told, "It's the baby." Applaud his tail wagging and being gentle. Make the event a happy one.

**110**  The big day that the baby comes home, make sure that Rover has been well exercised. Exhaustion will be your friend. Put four drops of Rescue Remedy in his water. As he hasn't seen Mom for a few days, she should come into the house solo at first. She looks and, more importantly, smells totally different, and Rover has missed her. Mom should spend as much time as necessary for Rover to settle down. She then goes out and gets the baby while Dad comes in and takes Rover out-doors (weather permitting), on leash, to meet the baby Mom is hold-ing. First impressions are the most powerful, so sweet-talk Rover's sniffing the newborn while shielding her face. It is important to allow him to smell the baby right away or the forbidden fruit of her will make him a pest. Rover's wearing a head halter should help ease an anxious parent through this initial hello. After a minute or two, offer Rover an extra-special treat, as if it were from the baby. Mom and Junior enter the house first and get seated and then the menfolk follow. Again, allow Rover to check out the baby, on lead, and now the baby gives him a toy or chew bone. Hopefully, Rover will go off and play with the toy. Leave a six-foot leash on him, though no one needs to hold it, to enable you to intervene easily if necessary. For safety's sake, I'd recommend leaving the lead on for at least the first few days, so long as someone is home, awake, and supervising, and *never* on a choke col-lar. You may even want to accustom Rover to dragging the leash around prior to bringing the baby home.

Keep Rover's (adapted) routine as intact as possible. Feed and walk him on schedule. It is natural for dogs to be attracted to stinky diapers. Expect him to be curious about the infant's vocalizations and somewhat stimulated by crying.

---

WARNING: Although it is extremely rare, occasionally a dog with a strong prey drive will be excessively aroused by the baby's squeals, it's as though they suggest to him that the infant is a wounded animal. He may point to the baby or squeal himself. His posture will be very forward and rigid, his ears and hair erect, his tail held high and eyes fixed on the baby. *This is very serious.* Keep the two apart and call a behavioral specialist immediately. Sometimes, through sys-tematic desensitization and counterconditioning, this preda-tory behavior can be resolved. Often, it cannot. *Additionally, if you have specific reasons to mistrust Rover around babies, I would recommend seeking professional help prior to intro-ductions.*

To minimize sibling rivalry, you need to demonstrate that the quality of your dog's life is enhanced, not diminished, by the baby. The more he is included in the baby's activities the less cause he will have for resentment. Rover will be thrilled that you are home more. Chances are there will be a lot of guests as well. Ask them to please take a minute to greet Rover and offer him a treat or toy before viewing the baby. The baby won't mind. You could even leave the goodies with a note outside the door. It typically takes five days for Rover to accept the baby as a keeper, and by the tenth day new patterns will begin to emerge. After six weeks, Rover will be hard-pressed to remember life without Junior.

Your next hurdle is when the baby begins to crawl. All of a sudden she's moving about, doglike, in Rover's domain, going places no man has dared to tread. Nothing's sacred, including Rover, as she will probably seek him out. In anticipation of the baby's mobility, begin to crawl around yourself, no matter how strange it seems. Although his reactions at this point are not a true barometer of how he will act when the baby crawls, at least you can start to desensitize him to this odd action.

Some dogs are afraid of the crawling. Others want to play. Occasionally a dog is even aroused—in the biblical sense. The fearful dog needs to be taught to exercise his flight option (versus fight or freeze). Establish a safe zone that Junior won't have access to and condition Rover to go there when feeling threatened (see the instructions on teaching GO LIE DOWN on pages 52–53). This is what I did with Monty when loud little boys came over. The dog who wants to play, though well intentioned, can inadvertently hurt the baby through rough pawing or mouthing. While you crawl around, should Rover initiate play, teach him that it is acceptable to play with a toy, not a baby. Toss his favorite toy, say, "Get your ball," and reward his doing so. If romantic Rover is not neutered, I'd recommend doing so. Otherwise, supervise him closely and verbally correct his humping. Once the novelty of Junior's mobility wears off, Rover will settle into new patterns.

**112**

**Don't for two seconds think that your dog would never bite the baby, or anyone else for that matter. Even the mushiest, most mellow mutt might bite a baby who pokes him in the eye or falls on his arthritic hip. He's not mean or bad. He is a dog. Never leave the two together unsupervised.**

Ensuring that old Rover accepts the new baby can be a lot of work. But, to quote my pregnant client Amy, "We'll do anything to make sure the two get along. If they don't, we'd hate to have to give away the baby."

## Kids and Dogs

I know of no more special relationship than that between a child and her dog. When they click, magic happens. Life's important lessons—tenderness, generosity, compassion, consequences, forgiveness, patience, and unconditional love—can be learned through caring for a dog. I truly believe that the best things about me came from being raised with animals.

So, if you are thinking about getting a puppy for the kids, don't. Get a puppy because *you* want one. If it works out well for your children, consider it a bonus. More often than not, puppies drive kids crazy, and vice versa. Puppies bite constantly, tearing kids' clothes and destroying favorite toys. The pup's jumping knocks the little ones over and can be frightening. We all have this Norman Rockwell image of a boy and his dog, and while that type of relationship may eventually evolve, it takes a lot of work.

Recently I got two calls from new puppy parents in a single day. The first was a mother whose four-month-old Great Dane Hamlet's mouthing is terrorizing her three daughters, the youngest of whom won't get off the kitchen table. The second call was about Diva, a ten-week-old Pekingese mix whose jumping makes it impossible for her to be in the same room as the son. Both of these mothers swore to me that the dogs they had grown up with never acted like this, which is doubtful. They seem to have been in doggy denial; this is what puppies do.

The addition of a puppy to a family can cause a lot of strife as family members determine who takes responsibility for what. No matter how intent your child is on caring for the newcomer, it has been my experience that the responsibility almost always falls on the adults. I am currently working with a family who has a feisty dachshund puppy, Diggity, and a six-year-old child, Melinda. During our lesson, the parents must have berated Mindy twenty times for mistakes made taking care of *her* dog. I thought the kid was terrific, yet her confidence was being squashed, as was Diggity's, by the parents'

**113**

unreasonable expectations. The relationship between a dog and a child should be fostered, not forced. I set Melinda up to succeed by presenting her with a small number of age-appropriate tasks: She would feed Diggity dinner, teach him to SIT, and brush him on Sundays. Mindy's share of responsibilities would increase in time and be duly noted on the "Doggy Do" chart that we designed.

## CHEAP TRICKS

Kids love teaching dogs tricks. I encourage this to keep them engaged. Here are just a few. David Letterman, watch out!

### Slap Me Five

This is SHAKE with attitude. Most dogs offer their paw naturally as a way of saying "Love me." Golden retrievers in particular are great at this. Whenever Rover paws at you, raise your hand to meet his and say, "Slap me five." You could throw in a "Bro" if you're so inclined. Give him a cookie and tell him what a brilliant boy he is. In no time at all, you've got a trick.

### Psychic Pet

This is a real crowd pleaser. With your best penmanship, write, "Wag your tail if you're a good dog" on a piece of paper and seal it in an envelope. Draw a paw print on the envelope flap as proof positive that it's really sealed (you wouldn't want anybody to think Rover's cheating). Tell the audience that your Rover has extrasensory powers. Hold the envelope up to your forehead, eyes closed, and in your nicest voice say, "Oh mystical one, demonstrate for me what is written in this sealed envelope." Da dum! Guess what your tail-wagging fool of a dog will do? Cavalier King Charles spaniels are excellent at this trick. If you have a Russian wolfhound or French bulldog, write it in Russian or French. I wouldn't try this with a Chinese shar-pei. If your dog is anything like my Stinky, you could write, "Wag your tail if you have bad breath."

114

### Jump Through a Hula Hoop

Wedge a hula hoop in a doorway that Rover usually walks through. It should be able to stay there on its own. For now, you want the bottom of the hoop to touch the floor. Every time Rover walks through it say, "Jump," and tell him what a good boy he is. Just leave it

**When kids and puppies are living together there are certain house rules that must be established:**

**1. Let sleeping dogs lie.** I'm guessing that whoever made this up did so because a child was bitten while disturbing a sleeping dog. Although an awake puppy might be very annoying to a child, she might be attracted to him when he is asleep. Managing this situation is tricky; you don't want to turn the kid off, but you also want to recognize Diggity's rights. I typically suggest that the kids be taught to read the sleeping pup a book or color a picture of him. Puppies grow up fast, and soon they'll need less sleep.

**2. Never crawl under a bed, table, or chair after Diggity.** Chances are that he's there because he wants to be alone. If Diggity's got something he shouldn't have, like your shoe, he may be guarding it and could try to bite you for invading what he sees as his den.

**3. Do not run after Diggity.** As mentioned in the COME section, this teaches him to run *away* from you.

**4. Greet the puppy calmly.** Shrieking, wild gesticulations, and backing up invite the puppy to jump.

**5. No hugging around the neck.** Most dogs hate this.

**6. It is absolutely against the law to ever hit or kick the puppy.**

there while your puppy's out and about for a few days, so long as it's okay with your parents. If Rover needs encouragement, you can crawl through the hoop yourself and hope he'll follow. Your sister or a friend could help you call him back and forth. Also, try tossing treats and toys through it. Remember to say, "Jump."

Once Rover is comfortable walking through the hula hoop, begin to slowly raise it a few inches a day. Let him feel good about jumping through the hoop when it is three inches off the floor before you raise it to six. How high you ultimately raise it depends on the size of your dog, of course. Duh!

After Rover has jumped through the hula hoop that's still stuck in your doorway for five days, try holding it in your hand and enthusiastically asking him to "Jump" through it. Yeah, Rover! If he tries to walk around it, practice this in a narrow hallway. Draping a towel over the bottom of the hoop will prevent him from crawling under it.

If for any reason Rover is scared of the hula hoop or if he's old or has sore hips, skip this trick. Just like some kids like to ride scooters and others want to play computer games, your dog may prefer to learn another trick.

**Roll Over**

Rover, don't.

# Afterword

## Dog Bless You

Stinky has cancer. He just turned seven last week. Unbeknownst to me, yesterday's biopsy was not to determine *if* the growth is malignant, but what kind of cancer he has. I think I chose not to know this. I'm still feeling numb, though not as shocked as you'd expect upon hearing such devastating news about one so young.

My Dinky Doodle Dog has been a mess his whole life. He was born one of eleven puppies to a stray who immediately attempted to kill her brood. My beloved friend Julie lovingly raised the litter from birth, a Herculean task by any standard. I picked the red puppy—the sickliest one—almost on a dare. "If that little Stinker lives, I'll keep him." He would have died at a dozen junctures but for Julie's dogged determination.

Feeling sad about having just lost my thirty-seven year old African gray parrot, Floozy, adopting the little stinker elevated my spirits. I named the puppy Prozac, but the nickname Stinky stuck. It suited him. At six months, Stinky was diagnosed with severe hip dysplasia. Then he had double cruciate ligament surgery at two. He was plagued with malabsorption syndrome and a degenerative eye disorder. Who knows? Maybe his dog mother sensed what was wrong. One could argue that the fragile puppy should have been allowed to die in infancy. And, intellectually, one might be right. But it is our hearts that dogs grab a hold of. It is our hearts that they break.

I have been down this road with too many of my dogs, though mercifully never with one so young. And I've held the hands of hundreds with dying dogs. You'd think it would get easier. You would be

**119**

wrong. Comments like, "He lived a good life" feel platitudinous in the wake of so huge an ache. Those words do more to ease the discomfort of the speaker than the mourner's pain. And shame on anyone who talks about "replacing" our dogs. Of course we can get another dog, but *replace* a hunk of our heart? I don't think so.

The lengths one goes to with a dying dog is so personal a decision that I would never presume to advise. What is right for Stinky may be wrong for Buddha. What I'm comfortable with may be uncomfortable for you. Then there's the issue of money. Losing Algunza, the pregnant German shepherd I found when a freshman in college and loved and lived with for fourteen years, was the most painful experience of my life. And I have many regrets surrounding her death. I regret having subjected her to a hideous surgery in lieu of letting go of her tired soul. I regret not having been with her when ultimately she was euthanized. It was for me, not Algunza, that I hung on, a mistake many of us make when dealing with our first life-or-death decision. I was with Mowgli at the end. I probably held on too long again, but the difference was that this time I didn't subject him to surgery or any unpleasant treatments. When it was P.J.'s time, my wise friend Julie, the person I go to with dog issues, suggested that rather than allow Petey's last days to be so brutal, and my remembering her suffering so, as death was imminent and inevitable, she deserved a more dignified good-bye. She was given one. With Monty it was easier. Perhaps less excruciatingly difficult is more accurate.

There is something so essential about grieving for a dog. All that is lost, after all, is love. As uncomplicated as his life is, so it is with his death. Don't apologize for your pain or deny it. Honor the love by allowing the agony. It's real. Find a way—your way—to memorialize him: Plant a tree, write a poem, make a donation—something.

It is the eve of my fiftieth birthday. In looking back over my life, many defining memories involve a dog (or two or three). I vividly remember the deep delight I felt when our dachshund, Bell—named for my Aunt Bell—licked the other side of my all-day lollipop when I was five. Uncle Herbie's airedale, Tara, curling up to spend the night at the end of the sofa I slept on made me feel like the most special person in the world. It didn't even matter that I later learned that it was *her* sofa. Then there was the time when I was ten that my parents called me to come home from Stephanie Burger's house, where I was spending the night. Although there had been no discussion about it, I hung up the phone, told Stephanie that we just got a dog, and ran the whole way home in my pajamas. Lady, the collie, was waiting. I met my late husband, Marc, walking our dogs—my two and his one—in Riverside Park in New York City. Our engraved wedding invitations read, "Algunza, Mowgli, and Rosie request the honour…" and their ceramic replicas topped the wedding cake. Marc committed suicide soon after we separated. I don't know how I'd have survived without Mowgli and P.J. to evoke happier times. In 1989, while flying home from Italy, an aneurysm ruptured in my brain. I attribute my miraculous recovery from the surgery and all that ensued to my dogs. An ICU nurse taped their photos to my many monitors. Whenever the pain or panic overwhelmed me, just looking at Mowgli, P.J., and Monty got me through. Though I often forgot my own name, I always remembered theirs. Reflecting on the tenderness with which Monty doted on me when I finally came home from the hospital still moves me to tears.

Absent from this book so far is mention of ReRun, my too-tall German shepherd mix. ReRun Rosengarten was the light of my life, my pride and joy. ReRun was the best thing about me. It has been a year and a half since ReRun died, and I just couldn't bring myself to write about him casually. Bless you, ReRun. This book is for you.

## Tribute to ReRun

"ReRun's gone."
Those words jolted me out of bed at 3 A.M.
Or was it 9?
The jet lag made it all the more surreal.
Thirty-six hours into France, Ronnie called:
"ReRun's gone."
I had to go home.

Why is it that when something that simply cannot make
any sense whatsoever—the abrupt death of someone
who embodied absolute goodness—that is when the
elusive illusion of sensibility matters most?

I didn't get to say good-bye.

I will never forget when Julie carried that three-week-old perfect puppy out for me to see. I fell in love. Just like they say mothers are supposed to upon seeing their newborns for the first time. Knowing, as I now do, that my own mother would have preferred not to have had me, perhaps there was much to make up for with this puppy born on my birthday. The light that emanated from his little soul—this baby Buddha—warmed me in a way I will feel forever.

"Just a dog," some will say
I resent being judged
As though there's a relative value to love
The heart has no hierarchy
It knows what it feels
Having buried my father, my husband, and more
I've learned that grief is generic
It is genuine. It's pure.
The agony of the last loss is compounded by those past.

I will always remember the Memorial Day parade when I carried eight-week-old ReRun down Main Street Westport for "Save Our Strays." The crowds that puppy drew. I have never been more proud.

There are those who believe we choose our time to die. I am not sure. Adi thinks ReRun chose to go while I was away to spare me. That would have been just like him.

Still the questions torment me:
Why on my first real vacation since my aneurysm blew up
flying home from the last?

Why while I was with Tom? In France.

Our much-anticipated tryst hardly had a chance.

How many thousands of lives did that gentle giant touch?

The catatonic woman in the nursing home who spoke only
    to ReRun

All those he delighted at puppy class graduations bedecked
    in that silly satin cap

His many TV appearances

That smile.


ReRun was the type of dog people who didn't like dogs
adored. The kind most wished theirs to be. Peggy said it
best: "ReRun was such a special soul; everyone who met
him recognized it immediately."
She was right.


ReRun was the only dog I've ever known to summer in
the bathtub. I never tired of watching his big old 105-
pound self play so delicately with Michelle, his pug girl-
friend.
Was it just last week that I caught him tiptoeing through
the living room with a pizza box in his mouth?
Just last week
ReRun, where'd you go?


ReRun Rosengarten

My pot of gold

My over the rainbow

Right here at home.


If the depth of one's love

Is measured by the depth of one's grief

Know, dear ReRun,

You were treasured beyond belief.
That I was not with you
When you died in your sleep
Has left a huge hole in my soul
That I will forever keep.

Thank you for loving me
You made me feel so special
I hope I was all you believed me to be
Thank you for gracing my life with your light
My guardian angel
I love you
Good night.

## Epilogue

I said goodbye to Stinky on May 6, 2002. In August,
I adopted puppy Déja Vu, "D.J." Life goes on.

# ACKNOWLEDGMENTS

Writing *Rover, Don't Roll Over* was surprisingly exhilarating. Never having written anything for public consumption before, I was totally captivated by this newfound way to express my love of dogs. Who knew? Getting started was the hard part. Actually, I'm not sure I ever would have begun if it wasn't for Mr. Raymond Hagel. While working with his Australian shepherd Maura, Ray commented on enjoying my training handouts and asked if I had ever thought about writing a book. "Only every day." Then, in addition to offering a number of sage getting started suggestions, Ray wrote something for me to read later. "Are you a writer?" I asked this older gentleman whom I'd only just met. "No," Ray said, "I was in publishing." I later learned he was the retired CEO of Macmillan, Inc. What had he jotted on that piece of paper? "Write how you want to be remembered." And that's exactly what I did. And did and did and did. Ray, your believing in me gave me confidence to believe in myself. You are my hero!

Okay, so I got a little carried away. After awakening at 4:00 A.M. seven days a week for eight months to write, it was time to try to sell what was beginning to look a lot like a book. Enter Jennifer Weis. My beloved friend Hedi Ann Lieberman (more about her in a minute) sat next to Jennifer at a Bar Mitzvah in New York. Jennifer just happened to be the editor at St. Martin's Press of the then best-selling novel *The Nanny Diaries*. Hedi told Jennifer about *Rover*, who in turn asked to see it. Ultimately, St. Martin's rejected the manuscript, but Jennifer said that she was going to "find a publisher for *Rover*," on her own time. And that's what this mother of four did. Wow! Only when Ten Speed Press expressed interest in the book ten months later did Jennifer finally agree to consummate our relationship and become my agent.

*And she's not even a dog person!* Jennifer, that you went so far out on a limb for a total stranger overwhelms me. (Do you believe we've still not met?) I owe it all to you.

Here's to Kirsty Melville, Nancy Austin, and Annie Nelson of Ten Speed Press. When researching the publishers to whom Jennifer Weis wrote letters accompanying the book, Ten Speed was my favorite. It felt like the best fit. Kirsty, that you of all publishers were willing to take a chance on my unsolicited manuscript was the most proud moment of my life. It filled me so that we could have quit right there and my tail would still be wagging! Nancy, your design is beautiful. Annie, I cannot imagine working with a more ideal editor than you. Your calm, gentle style is a perfect complement for my manic ways. Thank you Kirsty, Nancy, and Annie.

The following thank-yous to my fabulous friends feel woefully inadequate, but here goes:

Mark Basile: For reading the manuscript, for your sparkle and for Thanksgiving, I thank you.

Adelaide Bishop: Thank you for being ever ready to celebrate the book's many milestones. Love you tante.

Wendye Pardue: Your feng shui magic helped to transform my home into the peaceful space that allowed the writing to flow.

Melinda Philbrook: If not for your teaching me everything I know about computers, I'd still be scribbling *Rover* on loose-leaf.

Marie Runyon: It is an honor to know you.

Patty Volpacchio: Thank you for allowing me to write the Inside Poop, for reading the book, and your continued, enthusiastic support. You are a friend and a half.

Sylvia Wachtel: For reading the manuscript and always being there, I love you.

Special thanks to Julie: The most generous, supportive, and wise woman I know. What would I do without you? Julie, you are proof that guardian angels do exist.

Hedi Ann Lieberman: My agentette and best friend, this book is (almost) as much yours as mine. Thank you for introducing me to Jennifer Weis, for your extraordinary support, and for being the remarkable woman you are. You definitely deserve a raise!

And to my mother, Barbara Margolis, thank you for instilling in me in childhood a passion for dogs.

Extra special thanks to the following, without whom there would have been nothing to write:

Sammy Linn, Bunny Brody, Jody Ellis, Sydney Becker, Duke Cooke, Michelle Lawnsby, Boomer Freeman, Harry Thackaberry, Molly Miller, Zack Steigler, Channel Roth, Holly Craw, Partner Grannis, Roony Newman, Charlie Fein, Theo Howard, Cole Mitchell, Daisy Barker-Ruskin, Jasper Reitman, Owen Plunkett, Pinter George, Luna Sussman, Webster Marsh, Huckleberry Greenberg, Buffy Hilfiger, Lucy Gill Riley, Oisa Brault, Mariah Dibra, Clara Schnepp, Candy Wattell, Fiona Fleischli, B. G. Gordon, Taz Stierwalt, Sophie Garman, Miso Sherr, Scarlett Lenich, Buster McCorkindale, Mikey Naughton, Xarry McGuire, Jedi Steinberg, Buddy Tropin, Zoe Bible, Fergus Calder, Autumn Schilling-Connors, Abby Olean, Baxter Morse, Barco Elroy, Maddy Harris, Louise Ireland, Cara Feliciano, Max Conn-Scott, Ricky Laborie, Kate Ferarro, E tu Lichtblau, Cher Schwartz, Jacy Capetta, Angus Gorab, Midnight Petrasovits, Hagen Nelson, Addy Travers, Sara Lee Oladovich, Honey Luke, Buzz Neugold, Reilly Host, Daisy Grauer, Leo Klein, Chester Wasserman, Smudge Hough, Ashley Eisner, Casey Costello, Kris Cartmel, Maya Wasmer, Oscar Zeisler, Pearl Morton, Ella Rafsky, Fred Mombello, Polo Dupont, Tootsie Sorkin, Mutzi Kitt, Ruby Carlson, Arlo Ames, Cody Ellett, Max Friedman, Henry Rogart, Gracie Staverides, Bodhi Didato, Maxwell Jones, Tucket Hiltz, Bugsy Dresser, Opie Harding, Django Southworth, Molly Largay, Billa Landis, Juniper Chapman, Fuji, Samantha Labas, Zorro Lewis, Skip Dorrington, Ginger Brown, Kayla Lazarus, Frisco Sallick, Twizzler Spiesman, Jack Cohen, Bailey Bigelow, Dudley Armondino, Skylar Schulte, Cuspid Bialik, Matrix Albert, Gracie Sempler, Chance Bluestein, Billy Cole, Kirby Beasley, Midnight Schwab, Bailey Hunt, Aries Simmons, Cosmo Littman, Leopold Spitzer, Bell Hannon, Joey Ortiz, Honey Cardo, Duffy Church, Stuart Little Myers, Hunter Stringfellow, Jasmine Child, Phil Hall, Bravo Versus, Travis Tarshis, Bruno Grieves, Bella Scaright, Gert Epstein, Nana Rosiello, Lucky Loeb, Shipley Nelson, Rosie Grannom, Elvis Stampa, Maggie Oliver, Louie Minkoff, Lola Feral, Chester Hardy, Remi Blank, Sadie, Romeo Wachtel, Bonnie Runyon, Dakota Philbrook, Jilly Volpacchio, Dante Nelson, Wilson Basile, Bruce Pardue, Soubrette Bishop, Lev Lieberman, and all the little Rosengartens.

# INDEX

# the end . . . is the beginning